SON OF REBEL BOOKSELLER

A VERY LARGE HOMEWORK ASSIGNMENT

SAMUEL LATIES
ANDREW LATIES

Copyright © 2020 by Andrew Laties
Copyright © 2020 by Estate of Samuel Laties

All rights reserved. No part of this book may be reproduced, stored in a retrieval system, or transmitted in any form, or by any means, including mechanical, electric, photocopying, recording, or otherwise, without the prior written permission of the copyright owner.

Cataloging in Publication Data
Laties, Andrew
  Son of rebel bookseller—a very large homework assignment / Andrew Laties and Samuel Laties

ISBN 978-0-9971071-9-7
   1.   Booksellers and bookselling—United States.
   2.   Bookstores—United States. 3. Grief. 4. Loss (Psychology).
   5.   Business & Entrepreneurship. 6. College stores—management. 7. Laties, Andrew. 8. Laties, Samuel.

The events and conversations in this book have been set down to the best of the author's ability, although some names and details have been changed to protect the privacy of individuals.

"Sam Laties," by Samuel Laties, in *Liberated Learners,* Volume IV, Issue 7 (Amherst, MA: Northstar—Self-Directed Learning for Teens, 2003) 2-3. Reprinted by permission.

Cover design by Rebecca Migdal
Cover photo of Andrew and Samuel Laties, taken June 28, 1999 at World Trade Center, New York City

Printed and bound in the United States of America
First printing May 1, 2020
Published by Mythoprint Publishing
Easton, PA, USA, 18042

for Bec

On highest summits dawn comes soonest.
(But that is not the time to give over loving.)

      —Basil Bunting, *Briggflatts*

for Sarah

In spite of all their friends could say,
On a winter's morn, on a stormy day,
In a Sieve they went to sea!

      —Edward Lear, from "The Jumblies"

and for Dad (1926-2020)

Loveliest of trees, the cherry now
Is hung with bloom along the bough,
And stands about the woodland ride
Wearing white for Eastertide.

Now, of my threescore years and ten,
Twenty will not come again,
And take from seventy springs a score,
It only leaves me fifty more.

And since to look at things in bloom
Fifty springs are little room,
About the woodlands I will go
To see the cherry hung with snow.

      —A. E. Housman, *A Shropshire Lad*

CONTENTS

1—BIRTH 1

2—SING, GODDESS 3

3—MEMOIR OF A NIGHTTIME FANTASY 9

4—SAM CALLING 15

5—A BOY, A WEB SITE COMPANY AND A VERY LARGE HOMEWORK ASSIGNMENT: INTRODUCTION 19

6—INTO A MAELSTROM 21

7—A VERY LARGE HOMEWORK ASSIGNMENT: CHAPTER ONE—THE REALIZATION 31

8—PENT-UP FORCES 35

9—A VERY LARGE HOMEWORK ASSIGNMENT: CHAPTER TWO—AN IDEA THAT IN SOME PEOPLE'S MINDS MUST BE CARRIED THROUGH . 51

10—DOUBLE CONSCIOUSNESS 55

11—A VERY LARGE HOMEWORK ASSIGNMENT: CHAPTER THREE—THE WEB SITE'S FRONT PAGE 65

12—A VERY LARGE HOMEWORK ASSIGNMENT: CHAPTER FOUR—$5,000 DISCOVERED AND RELUCTANTLY USED 67

13—I WON'T BET MY SOUL TO THE DEVIL 73

14—A VERY LARGE HOMEWORK ASSIGNMENT: CHAPTER FIVE—ONE ELATED WEB SITE OWNER 113

15—MALPRACTICE 117

16—A VERY LARGE HOMEWORK ASSIGNMENT: CHAPTER SIX—SEEMINGLY STUPID IMMIGRANTS AND A REVELATION 123

17—OCCUPY PARK PLACE 127

18—A VERY LARGE HOMEWORK ASSIGNMENT: CHAPTER SEVEN—TWO FACE THE MORNING 131

19—OPEN HEART 135

20—CELL VS. SOUL: ON UNDERSTANDING PERSUASION 137

21—SAM'S COSMIC RIDDLE 141

ACKNOWLEDGMENTS 143

NOTES 145

> Admire his wings!
> Feel the fire at his neck and see how casually
> He glances up and is caught, wondrously tunneling
> Into that hot eye. Who cares that he fell back to the sea?
> See him acclaiming the sun and come plunging down
> While his sensible daddy goes straight into town.
>
> —Anne Sexton, from "To a Friend Whose Work Has Come to Triumph"

SON OF REBEL BOOKSELLER

1—BIRTH

BY SAMUEL LATIES, AGED THIRTEEN

Paint glides on, as my inner essence is being installed. Currents of thought begin to flicker inside my brain, in resemblance with a torch of light. Memories, what are they; a rose spurting out of the ground, becoming it again. A demolished citadel, left in total decay for all to see. A child falling, and falling, swirling with motion.

I am falling, I am that child. Down, down to a shallow hole of water, blue as ebony and ready to consume me; I cannot stop I cannot halt, I plunge and become alive.

I am in someone's arms. Squinting I can make up a person holding me. Where am I? Her face is happy, aged lines twinkle with delight at me. Far off in the twilight of my existence there is another person. Slowly the blur turns into a shape. First two blue lights appear; oval shaped and full of watery joy. They are pools, swarming like bees with liquid; I am drowning in them. Closing my eyes reveals a starry blackness. I am looking at stars, but of the mind. Losing consciousness, I am asleep.

SON OF REBEL BOOKSELLER

2—SING, GODDESS

MIDNIGHT, AUGUST 17, 2010

I woke on the exercise mat in Rebecca Migdal's brightly lit art studio with a crick in my back. The high-ceilinged loft's walls were covered with her surreal portraits and the illustrations for her graphic novels. Shelves displayed handmade dolls and puppets. The window-wall overlooking Holyoke Canal showcased starry night.

I'd met Rebecca three years earlier in Brooklyn, when my divorce with Christine Bluhm was finalizing. Rebecca was a writer, graphic journalist, puppeteer, and performance artist—her design and marketing company was R.L. Migdal Multimedia. She was also an editor for *World War 3 Illustrated*, the political comics anthology for which my Vox Pop coffeeshop partner Sander Hicks had once been publisher.

At the time, I'd been trying to finesse a move to Brooklyn, to work for Vox Pop full-time. Rebecca had felt I was being delusional, thinking I could step away from my twenty-year-old son Sam's daily care. She'd broken up recently, and decided to join me in Massachusetts—as it turned out sacrificing her job teaching digital illustration at Nassau Community College.

Rebecca had encouraged me to play my instruments again, and I'd rediscovered the musician I'd set out to become thirty years before. We'd been hosting rowdy monthly open mic salons in Rebecca's loft on the third floor of Paper City Studios, a hundred-year-old warehouse, playing a part, with dozens of other artists and activists, in the post-industrial revival of Holyoke.

I checked for the time on my black flip phone, but it was not powered on. I remembered I'd turned it off at ten PM, before falling asleep, because a collections agent was phoning repeatedly.

I pressed the power button. A text message appeared from my daughter Sarah, asking me to bring that bag of clothes to her boyfriend Alex's place. This meant we had to swing past the Upper West Side before going onward to pick up Rebecca's son Sylvan in Bed-Stuy, Brooklyn, then on to JFK Airport—I had swayed Sylvan into accompanying us with, "If you go to the weddings, you can skip the funerals."

Rebecca was at the computer, working concentratedly on her *Rosetta Stone* webcomic. She'd been at it for hours. Sylvan Migdal's own webcomic, the sci-fi comedy *Curvy*, had built up a fanbase tens of thousands strong over the past decade. Since last year, Rebecca had been using the online-publishing approach too, and tonight she was determined to get enough of her paranormal romance into the pipeline so that the webcomic could be fed out on schedule and her readers wouldn't have an interruption while we were in Seattle. I was about to warn her that, since the UWS detour would add forty-five minutes, we needed to leave Holyoke at four AM, so we should go home now and get some sleep—when the phone buzzed.

I felt a jolt of anger. Collections calling at midnight. The display on the screen didn't confirm this. It was a local area code and a familiar number. Cooley-Dickinson Hospital.

In the past few years, Sam's breakdowns had resulted in two separate weeks-long stints in the locked fourth floor mental health unit—that's why I knew the number.

I flashed on Sam, earlier in the day. Stopping at the house from Serio's Pharmacy in the late afternoon to drop off the refill of his anti-depressant, Nardil, I'd poked my head into his bedroom. He'd been sitting in his armchair with eyes closed—just where he'd gone when I'd dropped him off after driving him back from River Valley Counseling Center, an hour before. The boxed set of Homer I'd bought for his birthday was standing upright on his night table.

Over the past year, every night, Sam had broken his habitual silence for hours at a time reading great literature to Chris or me. The only words he'd spoken for the year had been Dickens, Hugo, Thoreau, Twain, Marquez, Dumas and Voltaire. Some of the most intense experiences of my life had been spent curled up on the living room couch under a blanket listening to his hours-long dramatic readings of Tolstoy's *War and Peace*.

It had started with Chris' idea to tell Sam that a doctor had prescribed he read a chapter of *David Copperfield* aloud each night. Surprisingly Sam had complied, speaking for the first time in six months. Since I generally only saw Sam during the day, I hadn't initially understood that this reading aloud was truly happening; Chris had finally convinced me to come over to the house one evening. Sam had opened *David*

Copperfield to chapter fifty-eight and read, with fluency and drama:

> It was a long and gloomy night that gathered on me, haunted by the ghosts of many hopes, of many dear remembrances, many errors, many unavailing sorrows and regrets. I went away from England; not knowing, even then, how great the shock was, that I had to bear. I left all who were dear to me, and went away; and believed that I had borne it, and it was past. As a man upon a field of battle will receive a mortal hurt, and scarcely know that he is struck, so I, when I was left alone with my undisciplined heart, had no conception of the wound with which it had to strive.

Since then Sam, Chris and I had each been involved in selecting the book Sam would read aloud next.

After all our years reading aloud to Sam as a kid, it was his reading aloud to us that was saving him.

Sam's obsessive-compulsive disorder had burst out as Tourette's tics and formulaic religious vows in fifth grade and morphed repeatedly. Social anxiety, anorexia, mutism. In fifteen years, there'd been recoveries and reverses, triumphs and setbacks: ten schools and thirteen doctors. "I've never seen this before," was the familiar refrain. One psychiatrist had scrawled the names of four antipsychotic meds onto a slip of prescription paper, instructing us to research these on the Internet and decide which we wanted to test. Sam's newest doctor had last week added the painkiller Oxycontin to the cocktail. Sam had indicated to Chris that he liked it.

I'd walked to the night table, slipped *The Iliad* out of its box, and said, "Hey Sam, you know what I would love, after we get back from the wedding next week, and Mom goes on her retreat? If you would read me *The Iliad.*"

I'd opened to the first stanza, and read aloud:

> The Rage of Achilles.
> Sing, Goddess, the rage of Peleus' son,
> Murderous, doomed, that cost the Achaeans countless losses,
> Hurling down to the House of Death so many sturdy souls,
> Great fighters' souls, but made their bodies carrion,
> Feast for the dogs and birds,
> And the will of Zeus was moving towards its end.

Sam hadn't moved, but there'd been a trace of a smile. I'd returned the book to its box with *The Odyssey,* hugged him around the shoulders, kissed him on the head, and said, "See you next week. I love you." I'd left the house and driven back to work at Eric Carle Museum Bookstore.

The black phone buzzed a second time.
"Yes?"
"Is this Mister Laties?" a woman asked.
"Who is this?"
"I'm calling from the emergency room at Cooley-Dickinson Hospital. Are you the father of Samuel Laties?"
Panic filled my chest. "Yes, I'm Sam's father."
"Mister Laties, I am sorry to have to tell you that Samuel is in cardiac arrest."
I was baffled. Then I understood and managed to ask, "Is he living?"
"Sadly, no," she said.

SON OF REBEL BOOKSELLER

3—MEMOIR OF A NIGHTTIME FANTASY

BY SAMUEL LATIES, AGED SIXTEEN

Soon I was to become a man, but not yet. In my fourteenth year, I was confined to a palace. I shunned all people, instead plunging myself into history. I had no friends and wanted none. A plague had been set at my door. I could not look at another human being. Horrible things might happen. I might crucify them. What if I raped someone? What if I mutilated them? What if I set them on fire and laughed hideously as they died? How can a person live like this? How can they live in the present if all that is there for them is despair? The answer is they can't. They, or at least I, had to live somewhere else, in the past. So I lived in the past and I built many houses there. One in ninth century Arabia, one in sixteenth century China, a few in Europe. Maybe a German principality somewhere. Maybe that principality needed an ambassador to the Imperial Senate. Me?

The Holy Roman Empire it is interesting to note was named after its predecessor, Imperial Rome. Rome had existed fifteen hundred years before it. I had more than a house there, I had a whole estate. I was a senator. I knew the emperor. I was the emperor. Rome was mine.

I had once been a pro-active child. In sixth grade (end of 1999) my parents were very proud. I ran a class newspaper. There were thirteen writers, submitting monthly articles to that publication. I also played in a jazz band, there were just four or five of us in it, I played trombone. It was great that way, I was the youngest one in Band, God, how I looked up to the older eighth graders. What's more, every couple of months we would get on stage and let the whole school know how good we were. All this culminated in December and made it my grand winter. The snows were Magnificent (with a capital M), I was Magnificent.

Then, in the early part of 2000, things started to go downhill. I started thinking people thought things about me. That I was a liar, or a fag, or a newspaper geek, whatever. No one thought this. It was in my head. On the outside, everyone saw that creative, colorful, friendly person that I had once been. Then they saw that color fade away. To them, I turned into a shadowy worry. That shadowy worry turned into a frenzied ghost. I could not gaze at people. I would hurt them.

The ghost with a soul still throbbing! But ghosts have no souls! Hear my confession Cardinal for I have sinned. Hear my confession, hear it, hear it! But I had never sinned. Only in my mind.

So, unable to cope with any work, in the state that I was in, I left school and retreated into my worldly palace, and then to my other homes throughout time. Gradually, even the continents looked different than the ones my parents saw. I had been swimming in a different sea for so long. Of course they looked different. I, the eternal wanderer was climbing different mountains and knew different, unknown oceans.

Stranded, I climbed out of the water and onto an unknown beach. With but a penny in my purse I climbed onto a cliff side and looked down. But, lo, there was a glorious city. In tattered rags, I surveyed this palace of desire. Temples to gods of lust.

SON OF REBEL BOOKSELLER

Amphitheaters of lions contesting. Shops of jade and gold and...
      Rachmaninoff. No, no. Not that yet. Not track six. Not Nicholas the Second. Repeat track five repeat.
      Where was I? In a Roman city. I knew the Roman Empire. Back in '45, with Julius in Tunis I had been here. That was a long time ago. The legions. The loot. This was different though. Bewildering. The old gods had been cast into the sea to sink on their own bronze. Devotion was receding in this Brave New World. Love thy neighbor...or what? Thou shalt not covet? Rampant capitalism is everywhere, why not get used to it? NO, I'll become a representative or senator. The President? I can change the world. The world needs to be changed.
      But that man over there, the one in the purple robe and curly silven hair. Grandeur sits upon his brow. Ancient to immortality he is. Ages past, mine own sought his company, sought to wick in his insulae. To light I looked; this was philosophy, ethics. I approach him once more, I call the bard.
      "Romulus, it is thine own companion, thy pupil."
      He turned, recognizing at once who called his name.
      "Augustus, by Venus, four-and-twenty years has it been?"
      I approach him. "You have not forgotten."
      "By Jove, the student that illuminated all my darkened galleries; my inner child. Vista brought me into this world once. You birthed me a second time."
      "Such praise, I don't deserve it. Whatever of me to your youth, my youth was enchanted into maturity by thee. I am but a starling to your great eagleity."
      "I must dissent. It was by your own efforts that turned me to the new. Teaching taught to you, in contrast to what you showed to me? Your sin is falsehood."

"You accuse me of sin. Yes, you are right, I am the better of us two. You taught me nothing wench. But of news, what has happened in this city since last I saw its changing streets?"

"Flamboyancy is the price of prosperity I fear. Thousandaires are like beetles now."

"Now you joke."

"No, shipping has launched its fleets. The world is a boat, on land and sea. Magnates groom their small ones in the shape of vessels. Slim at head and tow and fat in the middle. They must curve just so. It brings pleasure to their financing eyes. I have seen it, recently in fact."

"Have you? You have friends?" I gesture to the sky.

"Yes, just recently. One week ago my right eyelash was declared lordly. Tis be made a lord this day. The emperor thinks it noble. Carriaged he saw me and it. Looked upon it with wonder and proclaimed it peer-like."

"I see. You go to the palace now for ceremony?"

"Indeed, the emperor is in Tunis, away from his wife, so he may indulge in his hog-like devouring of food."

"She would not approve?"

"No. But ah, the palatial gates."

My guide ushered me through the gates of gold and turquoise and into the palace gardens. Here, it being almost evening, courtiers stood and gossiped. The women all wore men's wigs. The men, togaed and corseted, seemed to change their sex every few seconds. They then seemed to be inclined to invent new sexes that had not formerly existed. What perversity was this?

My guide urged me on through these crowds and on into the palace. It gleamed of ivory and silk. Hundreds of people were sitting on fur mats plunging their faces into massive pies, cakes and tarts. The emperor, at the end of this noble hall, was gluttonously embracing a bable cake. My companion led me on to the throne.

Sensing us, the emperor wrenched his head free of his delicacy and immediately shouted, "Usurpers!" All the diners in this hall immediately withdrew their faces from dessert. Togaed they shouted at me, "Our new Emperor, our new Emperor." The oriental women all immediately jumped on his former imperial majesty, crushing him. The men all hoisted me on to their backs and shouted, "Long live the Emperor, long live the Emperor!"

"I abolish slavery," I declared. The slave owners cheered. "I establish democracy," I shouted. The aristocrats cheered. "I institute a progressive taxation system culminating at eighty percent of annual earned income." Everyone cheered.

My eyes opened, vaguely I made out three AM on my bedside clock. It was golden. It was golden like my fantasies. "All my fantasies, they would amount to something someday," I thought. "Maybe in the future. Maybe when I get older, I'll amount to something. A senator maybe. A senator...a senator."

POST SCRIPT

Every nation's a world of kings
A crown of hair upon their heads

Some tyrants, some despots
Some Minoses and Fredericks

Civil wars wage in some
Ages gold are found in others

Each, power has,
Enumerated in their marbled eyes

Encumbered ministers some shall bear
Silver wisdom others hold

Territories vast and steep
Provinces narrow, cold and bare

Reflections of a greater world
Embronze their shapes on our beings

Format their reflections on ourselves
And sow, as kings the seeds of greater birth

As kings and queens stand all beings
Showing nations birth and death

Showing true monarchy as illusion
One God, as on Earth

Every nation's a world of kings
Every King a world again

4—SAM CALLING

READ AT THE SAMUEL LATIES MEMORIAL, AUGUST 2011

The year he had an apartment in Northampton I would sometimes check the browsing history on Sam's laptop, trying to get an idea what he was thinking about. It was always Supreme Court rulings and pages from the Harvard Law website. This was the 2008 fall semester when he had supposedly set aside the diplomatic and judicial career ambitions and retreated to a more realistic computer programming major. But his browsing history showed the dream was still alive. I wasn't surprised. It was only five years before that he'd told the Amherst High School counselor his aim was to one day be an ambassador. He'd told me at the time that his hero was peacemaker Richard Holbrooke, who'd negotiated the Dayton Accords.

But fall 2008 was just one year since Sam's month-long near-catatonic stay in the locked ward at Cooley-Dickinson Hospital, and he was still on two-hundred-fifty milligrams of Clozaril. The antipsychotic had freed him to return to college but exacted as price a fifty-pound weight gain, and, as it turned out, a dangerously increased tolerance for pain. Four weeks into the term what looked like a stomachache turned out to be a ruptured appendix. Sam had walked around holding his side for three days barely complaining, before landing in emergency surgery. That was his third emergency visit to Cooley-Dick in just over a year. I knew some of the staff by name.

After the appendectomy, Sam insisted on returning immediately to his apartment and his classes. He wanted the freedom. He walked in the woods behind Smith College. He watched movies he'd rented from Pleasant Street Video (the Kenneth Branagh *Hamlet*, five times, he said). Half asleep in bed he listened to Mahler, Beethoven and Rachmaninoff. Chris or I visited him morning and night, and drove him to doctor's appointments or grocery stores, but he'd rarely converse. He seemed locked in a battle with unseen forces. I'd only hear his voice over the phone, calling for a ride from Holyoke Community College when he missed the last bus to Northampton. On the car-ride I'd ramble about recent Supreme Court decisions or the upcoming election.

I was in school myself, mid-way through a Masters in Community Economic Development at Southern New Hampshire University, and I had a classmate from Rwanda who was an avid Barack Obama fan. I thought Jonas' optimism was misplaced, since the Republicans clearly controlled the voting machines. Driving with Sam to and from HCC that fall I expressed my pessimism about an Obama victory in face of certain vote fraud. I knew Sam was a believer in electoral democracy—he'd studied the extension of the franchise in Victorian England. Before he turned twenty-one—back when he still permitted himself to hike the trails around Amherst with me—Sam would revert to his old habit of discoursing on history, something he'd begun in 2000 during our walks along the Chicago lakefront when the foibles of Roman emperors were his favorite topic. As recently as those hikes in 2006 I'd been able to count on a lively discussion if I raised the topic of whether America had passed from democracy to fascism. I knew Sam believed in the possible triumph of right over wrong—and even good over evil—but by the fall of 2008 Sam's inner condition apparently mandated his outer silence, so my chatter in the car from HCC to Northampton about the hopeless corruption of our electoral system was usually a monologue. I knew his politics were more traditional and idealistic than mine; I could talk both sides fine.

Late on election night Rebecca and I were driving into Brooklyn. Our radio was broken so we didn't know what was unfolding. The streets in Bed-Stuy were empty but from apartment buildings we heard shouts and screams. At Sylvan's place we settled in front of the big-screen TV. Obama was ahead and America's usual very close call wasn't materializing. It looked like a clear victory.

My cell phone rang. I fished it out and checked the incoming number: it was Sam calling.

I was stunned. He never phoned except to ask for a ride from HCC.

"Hi, Sam," I answered.

"Dad," he said forcefully, "You have been so wrong."

I laughed. "You're right Sam; isn't this unbelievable? The vote was so lopsided they couldn't steal the election. Maybe sometimes democracy can work."

"Okay, well—bye," he said.

"Good-bye, Sam. Thank you so much for calling."

He was gone, and I found myself crying with relief, and hope: he was still the same old Sam.

I think Sam's beliefs about the mysteries of life and death were different than mine. I hope that he's right and I'm wrong about that subject as well.

SON OF REBEL BOOKSELLER

5—A BOY, A WEB SITE COMPANY AND A VERY LARGE HOMEWORK ASSIGNMENT: INTRODUCTION

BY SAMUEL LATIES, AGED TWELVE

There are many types of kids.

Some are interested in everything that moves. There are some that do all their work and they're just getting by, but what they are learning may be minimal. There are some kids who are obsessed with fashion on the outside and are really smart people on the inside. Of course, there are the geniuses in their own right also.

These are just some types of personalities, all different, all unique.

My main character in the beginning of this story has the worst type of personality you can have—he hates to learn, he has become a slave to popularity, and even though it is not described in the story it is pretty clear that he also likes to beat up anything smaller than he is. Over the course of the story he gradually changes into a more considerate kid, mainly because of something that happens in the story.

But I'm not going to tell you what that is here, you have to read the story.

6—INTO A MAELSTROM

DECEMBER 2011

In an apple orchard, bright expressionist murals in reds, yellows, and blues showed through the giant windows of a blocky, white, one-story building. The Eric Carle Museum of Picture Book Art, founded by the author of *The Very Hungry Caterpillar*, looked like one of Carle's books: dramatic colors in tranquil white space. Through the tall glass entrance doors to the right was the bookstore I helped launch in 2002. I was ringing a customer at the cash register when this email appeared on my iPhone, on the shelf beneath the cash desk:

> FW: AVAILABLE POSITIONS AT PARK PLACE COLLEGE. CHILDREN'S BOOK STORE MANAGER AND BUYER
> you should take this job and move to new york
> Sarah Laties | Assistant
> Every Child a Reader

I'd labored under a cloud of grief for the sixteen months since Sam's death. Meanwhile, Vox Pop had collapsed, victim of our own ambition, the recent financial crisis, and the gentrification we'd stimulated. I had tried to distract myself by completing the revision of *Rebel Bookseller* and doing a book tour, but I was depressed; moping evenings and sleeping a lot.

That night Rebecca and I discussed whether moving to New York and undertaking a new, challenging job might help me. I began to develop a feeling that Sam would have wished me to make this effort.

Chilly dusk.
Vibrate. Two steps up from the sidewalk to the covered front porch of my Eric Carle Museum boss Alix Kennedy's college-town Victorian. I rooted in my pocket. Two-one-two area code: Manhattan. "Bec, I need to take this."
Vibrate. Rebecca, opening the front door to the staff party, called back, "See you inside."
Vibrate. Three steps down I squeezed onto the street between parked cars as Kristin and Steve passed. "Up in a sec," I said, rubbing the glass iPhone display. "Hello, this is Andy."
"Mister Laties?" A Jamaican woman's lilting accent.
"Yes, who is this?"
"Vera Stringer, from Park Place College. I need to schedule your interview. What days work next week?"
"The job's open?" I had applied six weeks earlier and heard nothing. "I leave the country Monday and I'm not back till February. I'm consulting for a bookstore chain in Bangkok. Can we do it after I return?"
"The search committee is eager to advance this. A member is scheduled for surgery on the third."
"How about by phone? I can call from the hotel."
"There are seven members. Let me get back to you."

Two weeks later I was dialing in to a conference call. I had food poisoning and was feeling draggy. Still, I had managed to put on a show for my Thai clients. Several days and thousands of dollars into this gig advising the Asiabooks chain on their children's bookselling strategy, I was even starting to think that maybe I could sell such services to other clients globally.

Managing Director Sirote Jiraprayoon had read *Rebel Bookseller* a few months before. He'd liked it so much he'd hired me to coach his buyers and lecture to his managers. When we met in person, he'd told me English language children's book sales were booming in Asia and bookselling was a "blue-sky business"—full of opportunity.

So, could this consulting job springboard me into a new phase? To be simultaneously applying at Park Place Bookstore in New York was to place two sharply different life trajectories side by side.

The call went through. As Rebecca listened, sitting on the hotel bed, I commenced an hour-long interview with the seven-member search committee. The conversation was led by Vice President Vince Tower. I did my best to project energy, enthusiasm and optimism.

I was asked if I had ever managed a union workforce before. "No, but I used to be a member. I was the only shakuhachi player in the Chicago musicians' union."

How much salary would I need?

"You've got two jobs posted: manager and buyer. But I'm my own buyer. So, a hundred thousand for both jobs?"

"We can do that," Vince Tower responded.

I felt a surge of confusion, and barely kept myself from blurting, "Really?"

I was asked what I thought about the fact that the bookstore was losing two-hundred-thousand dollars per year. I said, "I run my bookstores for profitability."

I was informed there were three years left on the lease.

I concluded the interview on a self-assured note, hung up, turned to Rebecca, and inhaled deeply.

"How do you think it went?" she asked.

"Well, I wouldn't have to split the job with someone else, and they'd give me the salary I'd hoped for. But the store's been losing money for a while."

"Sounds like you'd have your work cut out for you."

"True." My mind was reeling, and I didn't say anything, just watched her slipping on her sandals,

"So, before we head downtown, I need to go buy some more white gouache." She began to explain the route to an art supply store she'd located, not too far from our hotel. While I was at work, she'd been painting poster art: a portrait of Nobel Prize-winning eco-activist Wangari Maathai. "Let's just go grab a bite at the buffet first," she urged. "But take my advice and stay away from the shellfish bar!"

As I laced up my sneakers, I felt elated and exhausted. Was this what Sam had in mind for me?

The Park Place search committee members—individually and as a group—conducted additional interviews, and during this process I learned there was a way forward. A relationship had been established with a rapidly growing chain of charter schools. Conquest Academies was spending hundreds of thousands of dollars with Park Place Bookstore—so much that the retail store's entire annual loss would this year be offset by the profits from this wholesale channel.

In late February I received an email from Vince Tower telling me I was hired. A week later a letter came from college president Amelia Wright. I was welcomed to the Park Place family and offered a salary of ninety-eight-thousand dollars, with a five-thousand-dollar bonus if I achieved the goal of cutting the bookstore's annual loss in half. I was to concentrate on digital initiatives: President Wright wanted me to develop a successful e-commerce business, as we'd done at

Eric Carle Museum Bookstore, where half our sales were online.

Vice President Ben Daniel had informed me during the interview process that President Wright had the previous fall sent out an email announcing that Park Place Bookstore was likely to have to close due to persistent losses, and this had elicited a furious reaction from many parents in the Park Place School for Children. I understood that my hiring had taken place in this political context. So, I was nervous about my welcome letter's focus on digital initiatives. However, I assumed President Wright intended to give me some time to get the storefront back to viability.

What concerned me most was how I would go about managing the Conquest Academies account. I believed in progressive education. Every child is unique; children's interests should be respected, stimulated and nurtured; teachers should be honored. My research online suggested Conquest Academies' disciplinarian approach and disrespect for teacher professionalism represented the opposite philosophy.

Most offensive to me personally: I knew that some families to whom publicly funded charter schools offered opportunities had to withdraw their kids, because they couldn't keep up the pace. Having been the father of a so-called "special" kid, I felt strongly that schools receiving taxpayer funds should be obliged to bend over backwards to support their troubled students, and not permitted to simply shed "underachievers" the way private schools could.

Sam is twenty months old and speaking a few words at the time Sarah is born. Then, he stops talking. Still, a year later, although he understands what you say, he does not speak.

The doctor advises we enroll him in preschool. Among other children his language will emerge.

A home daycare operator who frequently brings her kids to storyhour at The Children's Bookstore tells me she has an opening. Chris, Sam and I go to a nice Colonial in the Lakeview neighborhood on a weekday morning. About ten kids are there, including the host's two boys.

We head down to the basement, which is set up as a playroom. Our host's older boy, who is six, acts bossy with the three- and four-year-olds.

The host gathers the children, but Sam begins to run around the space, knocking items off shelves. Chris and I fail to catch him—he is difficult to subdue. As we strive to contain his erratic behavior, the host takes a book from her high bookshelf: Leo the Late Bloomer. She tells her attentive kids that Sam is simply a late bloomer, and she reads them the book.

Sam becomes interested in the reading, and we all sit through it. Afterward, the host invites Chris and me outside. In the narrow passage next to her house, she tells us Sam is "special." She will not be able to accommodate him.

She never appears with her group at The Children's Bookstore's storyhours again.

A few days later, I ask a different home daycare provider who's been bringing her kids to storyhour if Sam might be welcomed into her group. She says she has an opening, and we should stop by.

At this house, in Logan Square, the program is on the main floor, encompassing living room, dining room, den and two bedrooms. The walls are lined with low bookshelves. There are hundreds of books; many seem to have come from our store. The titles are well chosen, and strikingly multicultural. The children are selecting books freely.

The host, BJ Richards, has her own child here, but this time it's a three-year-old daughter. Also in the group is the daughter of the house's owners Judi Minter and John Ayers.

Sam clearly likes it, and he is invited to join. The following week—although separation is difficult—Sam's beginning at BJ's Kids seems to be going well. Then a week later, BJ reports that Sam has begun to speak to her and the other children, using elaborate sentences.

His separation anxiety vanishes.

It's terrific to be able to talk with Sam. BJ loves him and appreciates his thoughtful, considerate nature. He is affectionate to the other children.

The following year, Sarah excitedly joins him there.

I learn BJ's story gradually. She is a practitioner of anti-bias education. She launched her daycare in New York City, where John Ayers' older brother Bill worked for her; Bill's sons were attending BJ's, too. Meanwhile, Bill was getting his Masters at Park Place College; he later wrote a book—To Teach: The Journey of a Teacher—that featured BJ.

Bill Ayers is now a professor of education at University of Illinois, and he'd helped arrange for BJ to move to Chicago and run her daycare out of John and Judi's house.

In the '90s, John Ayers, while executive director of the Civic Committee of the Commercial Club of Chicago, became a leading player in the early charter school movement, often in collaboration with his brother Bill's innovate graduate students. Now, in 2012, I sought John's advice, writing, "I am heading into a maelstrom. I am leaving Eric Carle Museum and going to manage Park Place Bookstore, in NYC. Park Place currently is doing a huge contract job with Conquest Academies, which is a controversial, rapidly expanding charter school operation. I will be dealing with Conquest Academies quite a bit, very soon. It's especially ironic that Park Place College—which is unionized—is doing lots of business with Conquest Academies—which is a non-union thorn in the side of the AFT. I am coming in as the non-union (because managerial) supervisor of nine unionized bookstore workers. I need some help orienting!!"

John responded, "Hey, I love that bookstore. You will do well there. And living in NYC will be fun for you. Love the version of you as a rapacious capitalist manager driving the union workers for increased productivity. I know a bit about Conquest Academies, but not a lot. It is run by Linda Lasch, a former pol who is a fierce critic of bureaucratic schooling. She's aggressive in the extreme and well-funded. I explored a top position with her organization in 2009, but the fit felt wrong; her negative personality was too hot and her rhetoric too unbridled. She had big bucks—hedge fund dollars, I think, and a corporatist analysis of American schooling. Linda has the money and the intelligence to go get the support of the best, which in NYC is Park Place. I have no other insight into the schools. Many charters become test prep factories and can churn out good numbers, but the lasting educational value is questionable. I really don't know if they are like this. Let me know what you learn."

I arranged a six-week transition, going into New York one day each week for training with longtime bookstore manager Myra Raines, who I'd known professionally for years. During this transition, I kept asking Myra to arrange for me to shadow our Conquest Academies account supervisor Jan Smart. I knew Jan's eighteen years at Park Place Bookstore helping teachers select books for their classrooms underpinned extensive knowledge about the uses of children's literature in school settings. Somehow my Conquest Academies account training was not forthcoming, even though Jan was always onsite: she was operating the wholesale division—called Bulk Orders—out of a room at the back of the upstairs.

Finally, Jan wrote in an email that she would be reporting not to me, but to Vince Tower directly.

The implication was worrisome. Elements in the college bureaucracy could be preparing to close the unprofitable retail bookstore but continue servicing the profitable Conquest Academies wholesale account.

The transition was over. Myra left, and I assumed management. President Wright had invited me to make a brief strategic planning presentation to the entire forty-member Park Place Board of Directors. At the meeting, which took place at a rural conference center, I spoke of sharply extending the store's hours of opening—from eight AM to ten PM, seven days a week—while hugely building its marketing campaign to six hundred events a year.

I encountered a highly conditional response hedged with doubt from several vocal trustees who I later learned were powerful figures in the world of New York real estate. One spoke of his friendship with Barnes & Noble owner Leonard Riggio. "Even Lennie wouldn't take over our store. I asked him to!" Another said, "I support these experiments. This is what we should have done years ago. But we've got to see results quickly. If this doesn't work, then come on. What about Amazon and e-books? Let's be realistic. Why are we holding onto this store?"

Trustee Albert Rollins, a member of the bookstore oversight committee who was seated next to me at the oval of two dozen tables, whispered contrarian advice: "You'd better start looking for a new location."

7—A VERY LARGE HOMEWORK ASSIGNMENT: CHAPTER ONE—THE REALIZATION

Jason drifted into his house with his parents and went up to his room.

He had been at another party. There were so many of them these days. He did not regret going to them, after all, they were fun.

His room was a regular kid's room, posters of his favorite movie stars on the walls, a desk for school, which had gotten so dusty that when you put a fan next to it and turned it on, it looked like a snowplow spitting snow in all directions. Then there was his bed. A simple, regular bed.

His eyes lingered on the desk. He remembered his Mom buying it for him, saying he didn't have a place to work and he needed one.

He despised that word: work. And he hated doing it. He was much better at socializing and going to parties.

There was something he had to do.

Normally he would just blow off his homework assignments, but he remembered that for some reason, this was more important.

He wracked his brain. What was it?

It probably didn't really matter anyway.

Slowly he got up and walked to the door, opened it and closed it with a slam. He walked down the stairs with a clippity clop motion, and went straight for the computer, and inserted the disk to the new video game which he had bought the other day.

The game loaded up and an alien appeared on the front of the screen and said, in a very deep voice, "What do you want to do?" A couple of options appeared. The highlighted and capitalized one was "PLAY NOW."

Jason yawned and clicked.

The screen said Level 1, and he started shooting aliens.

Part of his mind was on the aliens, but part of it was slightly worried.

What was it?

There was something he had to do. But he did not remember what it was.

What was it?

What was it?

There was a hideous laugh, and the big alien reappeared on the front of the screen and said that Jason had lost, and that it would be best if he tried again. Jason decided not to play again because the feeling of haunting uncertainty which had been growing over the last ten minutes was now at a bursting point.

What was it?

"Now," Jason said, out loud. "I'll sort this into categories. I know it's not to do with a party, or something to do with my social life. It can't have to do with my parents because they never ask me to do anything, except clean my room and do my homework. It couldn't be anything to do with school, because I blow off 99.9% of all my assignments. So why would I care about this?"

It was a complete mystery.

What could it be?

He tried to make himself remember, yet nothing came.

This was weird. Maybe he was getting that disease that old people get when they forget everything.

Or maybe he was just making it all up.

That was probably it. He was just making it up.

Yeah, why should he worry. His mind was just making it up. And there was nothing wrong at all. That must be it. There was no other explanation.

Jason sighed a deep breath of relief. His heartbeat got slower.

"That was scary," he said out loud, and shook his head.

Suddenly he realized that there was something.

Jason's heartbeat tripled.

Then he realized what it was.

His heartbeat quadrupled.

It was the project that all his other classmates had been intently working on the entire year. It was entitled, "The Detailed Study of Cultures, Migrations, and Civilizations of the Last Ten Thousand Years."

This project was supposed to be approximately one hundred pages long, and it was due tomorrow.

This was too much for Jason's poor heart. For now, it had quintupled its normal speed. It must stop, and there was only one way this was going to happen.

By fainting, so that's what he did.

8—PENT-UP FORCES

Morningside Heights. After ten years running Eric Carle Museum Bookstore in a setting so bucolic it belonged in a calendar—an apple orchard in the shadow of the Holyoke Mountains—now I was spending my days and nights staring out on Broadway, one of the busiest streets in the world. The humanity, the vehicles, the noise—Preacher John strolling up and down each evening calling, "I love you! I love you! I love you!"

Standing at the bookstore check-out counter, my view across the street was of Tom's Restaurant, the classic Greek-style, twenty-four-hour, cash-only diner made famous by the '90s TV sit-com *Seinfeld*. So famous, that the actor who had played the character Kramer now ran a tour business that every day deposited selfie-taking tourists in front of the iconic eatery.

The most time I'd spent in the neighborhood had been in the summer of '78, when I'd played street music on weekends. My high-school underground newspaper friend Bill Meade was attending Manhattan School of Music; I'd crash at his place on Cathedral Parkway. We'd sometimes get breakfast at Tom's.

Rebecca and I figured out we'd crossed paths in Morningside Heights in the summer of '78. She'd arrived from California in August to stay with her boyfriend Rodd in his father Hector Elizondo's apartment at 107th and Broadway.

Bill Meade, now a big-league theater producer, still lived nearby. He'd stop in with his twin sons, Henry and Patrick, his wife, Judy, and the family dog. I loved reminding the eleven-year-olds they were the age their dad and I had been when we'd met in 1970.

Sarah was also around: her boyfriend lived on 106th—they'd met the summer of 2005, in the Columbia Creative Writing Program. When Sarah walked past with Alex, and they waved at me through the window as I was ringing a customer, that moment was reason enough for having taken the job.

But also, another luminous memory hovered.

An unseasonably warm February weekend. Chris, Sam, Sarah and I have driven from Amherst into New York City. Fifteen-year-old Sam loves dramatic architecture: I suggest he and I visit the Cathedral of St. John the Divine. On exhibit there, we discover hundreds of exquisite woodcuts from Barry Moser's wildly ambitious, seriously unorthodox Pennyroyal Caxton Bible. *Afterward, we drift down 112th Street to Park Place Bookstore. We browse for an hour.*

I was determined to stay open till ten o'clock every night, to capture the restaurant-goers on that crowded street. Most of the staff I'd inherited were not interested in working these new hours, but one did agree to. Lucy was twenty-three, energetic, and full of children's book knowledge.

Also, the higher-ups at the college had agreed to let me bring in a new part-timer. Sylvan Migdal's girlfriend Jessica Spears, who'd recently completed her Masters in Library Science, had offered to help. I arranged with Jessica to work six to ten, alongside Lucy, three nights a week.

On Jess' first day, I said, "Lucy, I'm thinking Jessica can learn the register by standing behind you while you're ringing."

Lucy was alarmed. "You're the only one who can train."

"Well, this is how I'm suggesting to train her—she can observe for a while, and then she can ask questions."

As Jessica stood silent, Lucy began to lecture. "Managers train; not me. It's in the contract."

The contract. I had been shown the fifty-page union contract by Myra Raines during the transition period. Job titles were part of the contract, and a couple of sentences described the duties of each job. Lucy was a full-time bookseller, level three. It had not occurred to me that her duties were exclusive. She was supposed to perform only the specified functions. The premise was that she should be earning more money if she had additional duties.

In every store I'd run before, everybody did everything. Now I began to learn that at Park Place, the only people to whom that principle applied were managers and part-timers. The full-timers I had inherited were all union booksellers, and none of them were permitted by contract to show anyone how their jobs were done.

I trained Jessica myself.

A few days later, in the evening, Lucy settled into an informative disquisition. "You can't just bring in a new part-timer and put them on the register. At Park Place, we do forty-five days of training first."

I was shocked. "Forty-five days?"

"I was trained for forty-five days—I wasn't allowed to talk with a customer or touch the register."

"Who trained you?"

"Jan."

"What did Jan do with you for all that time?"

"I had to learn where everything in the store is—the whole shelving and category system—I had to memorize the policies and procedures—how to do special orders—I was reading classics and new titles. I was tested. Finally, I was allowed to start working with customers."

I had never heard of such a training regimen in a bookstore. "Was everyone here trained that way?"

"Yes—Jan trained all of us."

"So—overall, what did Jan do, when she was managing?"

Lucy laughed warmly. "Jan did everything. She told everyone what to do, where they should be, all the time."

"What about Myra?"

"We almost never saw Myra. She was always in the buying office, with the door closed. When Myra came out onto the sales floor, we'd all be like, 'Myra!'"

"You were scared of Myra?"

Myra Raines, at age sixty-five, stood five feet tall, had white hair, wore wire-rimmed glasses, and looked like a young grandma. She projected a New York toughness: dressed in black, filled with wiry energy. She peppered her speech with a full range of Yiddish.

"Not scared, just, like: It's Myra!"

I began to understand that Myra's employees had worshipped her.

True: she'd read seemingly every children's book and could talk about them all brilliantly. I'd never approached her level of children's lit erudition.

Kindergarten, according to fourteen-year-old Sam. From "My Schooling," written for the online school, Clonlara.

My schooling began when I was six.

I went to kindergarten at the Chicago Waldorf School, where we employed our time in such activities as building towers of blocks and drawing pictures of whatever came into our imaginations. We romped up and down the classroom talking, jumping, singing, and playing and then, after a period of time, would be called into a circle to chant rhymes and listen to stories. We all had roles; there were the hoarders of crayons, the bangers of drums, there were the cart-wheelers, the story maker-uppers, there were the blanket-hanging engineers and the army lieutenants, there were the knitters and readers, the bouncers and wreakers, the singers, the dancers, the unicorns; the tribal warriors, the babysitters, the demigods. There was a little bit of everything.

Now, when I look back on it all in retrospect, I realize that I wasn't part of the scheme as much as I should have liked. Yes, I suppose I was the multi-versanal timekeeper, with my new waterproof watch (it's 10:36 AM everybody, it's 10:36 AM). I suppose I did make sure that all the arctic expeditioners were aware that they had discovered the North Pole at approximately 10:36 AM, or had Lancelot recognize that it was at 10:36 AM he had saved Guinevere and not at 10:37 AM, but on the whole I think somewhere inside me I would have dearly liked to go out and make a friend but somehow couldn't, a reoccurring social pattern in my life.

A week later Lucy told me, "I'm going to work for Diane Wolkstein on her storytelling festival. My last day is next week. I already talked to H-R."

I said, "That's a great opportunity! It's terrible for the store, but New York definitely needs a storytelling festival."

Lucy didn't seem as excited about the festival as I was. This confused me, and I contacted the human resources director, Norma Rendell, and arranged to meet with her.

Norma had been a member of my search committee. On the ninth floor of the college, in the office at the back of the H-R suite, from behind her desk, Norma drily informed me, "Your employee Lucy does not think much of you."

Norma handed me Lucy's three-page exit interview. This itemized my many faults.

"This woman is my daughter's age. Only my daughter should be allowed to say things like this about me."

Norma shrugged. "Good luck with those people. Myra created a whole little world over there."

"My Schooling," after kindergarten.

First grade was a new and exciting experience. I remember anxiously walking in on the first day not knowing what I would find, thinking it might be scary and different. These fears had soon vanished when I beheld the myriads of children in class drawing and then hurrying between desks, showing the pictures that they had created to one another and excitedly running back to their workplaces to produce more of them. After being told that this was drawing hour I settled down at my own desk and began to draw.

But what does one make when creating pictures? What was there to make, to draw? A stop-sign along a road, I drew that; a tomato patch, I drew that too; an oversized beetle, I drew that as well. The possibilities were endless, and my drawing book was soon filled up to the brim. I was in need of a new one, and another one after that. I was emotionally integrated into the classroom like a bee in a hive and I found that what I had assumed would be a frightening experience was really, a quite enjoyable one.

SON OF REBEL BOOKSELLER

> *In Waldorf, the student remains in one class for eight years. He gets to be closely acquainted with his teacher and fellow pupils and thus a bond of friendship and trust develops. In this environment, I soon made friends and my little ego slowly began to grow.*

We completed our full, all-staff count of the physical inventory on July second. Now I was ready to begin my big effort at transforming the store to make it more welcoming to families. I'd outlined my idea to Myra in an email back in March: "I am wondering if you have ever experimented with what is essentially a complete inversion of the location of the sections relative to the store floor levels. That is: have you ever had Picture Books and Fiction on the second floor, with Science and Arts on the first floor? Cushions and chairs all around. Try to go for maximum coziness."

Myra had responded, "Our bread and butter in children's books is picture books and fiction and you risk losing the casual shopper who won't make the trek upstairs."

For several months, I'd done what I could to persuade the staff that we should experiment with a different store layout. None thought it was a good idea.

In July, I hired a new part-timer and the two of us set about the reorganization, over the full-time staff's objections. We moved every category. Fiction came upstairs—though we did leave picture books at street-level. The process took weeks. Thankfully Zack Overton got impatient and pitched in.

The upstairs was now less a professional education bookstore and more a huge living room filled with children's literature. The parents and children adapted immediately. We got a lot of compliments. But the teacher customers were upset. Their sections were crammed into the rear area: my analysis had shown these professional resource books were selling more slowly than in years past. This was of course the impact of Amazon, siphoning off business by selling these expensive books at a discount. The teachers who yelled that I was destroying their bookstore had not been buying enough from their sections, and I told them so.

"My Schooling," trouble comes.

The process of schooling started with mostly stories and rhymes and over the next couple of years gradually became more and more mentally minded, it was focused more and more on technical aspects. The early years were full of tales of many cultures and religions. In second grade, we focused on Christianity, in third grade Judaism, but by fifth grade vexatious math problems I didn't understand were being thrown at me right and left. To boot, by fourth grade my OCD had begun to show, and I became entangled in a flurry of secret religious obsessions; continuous and rather ridiculous vows to God. Near the end of fifth grade my parents finally came to the conclusion that I should be removed from Waldorf. I learned practically nothing that year—as my religious obsessions sapped all my energy—and so it was considered necessary that I repeat fifth grade, but in a different classroom and in a different school.

I received an angry email from Vince Tower demanding to know if I were stocking pornography.

Vince had received an anonymous packet including Xeroxes of pages from books now on the shelves. These depicted nudity and sex.

In addition, the packet contained detailed complaints about my behavior and the effects of my new policies on staff and customer morale. Vince's email said that he would bring me the packet later in the day, but he wanted all explicit material off the shelves immediately.

I emailed that I had—as I'd told him I would—brought in an assortment of illustrated books for adults: the same excellent titles I had been selling at Eric Carle Museum Bookstore. I'd shelved this "Picture Books for Grown-ups" section at adult eye-level. It was designed to appeal to the Columbia University crowd strolling Broadway in the evening. These books were not pornography. They included acclaimed graphic novels, art books relating to children's literature, and crossover humor such as the adult work of Edward Gorey, Tomi Ungerer, and Shel Silverstein.

That evening, Vince strolled into the store and tossed me a battered interoffice envelope. It contained several pages of complaints. I was dismissive, I was brusque, I wasn't listening. I'd reorganized the displays although staff had protested. The new storyhours, puppet shows, author readings, concerts and art workshops were attracting crowds that prevented shoppers from accessing bookcases. The longer days stretched hour-by-hour staffing levels too thin, forcing staff to achieve more than was feasible, and undermining their freedom to take time recommending books to readers.

Most startling were the Xeroxes.

From *Is Sex Necessary? Or, Why You Feel the Way You Do*, by James Thurber and E.B. White, published in 1929, a cartoon of a man with a nude woman slung over his shoulder, a faint line delineating the woman's ass-crack.

From *Fun Home,* the National-Book-Award-winning graphic novel by Alison Bechdel, a panel showing a woman's face approaching the crotch of another woman.

From the back cover of the current censorship-themed *Expression! Repression! Revolution!* issue of *World War 3 Illustrated,* an image of a severed hand with Arabic script above it. Blood poured from its wrist, the middle finger curled up, and all the other fingers had been chopped off. This was the work of Egyptian political cartoonist Ganzeer and referred to the government crackdown during the Arab Spring.

And shouldn't I have predicted, a page from Rebecca Migdal's self-published *Cock Robin's Wedding*, her surrealist, Greek-myth-inspired graphic novel. The god Eros is bouncing the skimpily dressed goddess Artemis on his knee, to her annoyance. I'd put this onto the shelf without consulting Rebecca first.

Rebecca's presence in the store had caused irritation among the staff. Her company R.L. Migdal Multimedia was doing things none of the booksellers could, because of their union contracts with explicit job descriptions, not to mention a lack of relevant expertise. The team Rebecca had assembled was building a new website. They were filming videos of all events for a new bookstore Youtube channel. One freelancer was supervising the explosive growth of Facebook and Twitter accounts. Two others were producing frequent e-newsletters. Rebecca herself was performing well-attended fairy-tale themed puppet shows every Saturday.

On her own time, in her life as an editor for *World War 3 Illustrated,* Rebecca had been writing and illustrating the article "In Praise of Whistleblowers" for the censorship issue. And she was just completing work on "Village Days," a chapter for Paul Buhle's historical graphic novel anthology, *Bohemians.* "Village Days" was about Greenwich Village in the early years of the twentieth century—coincidentally the time and place of Park Place's founding—focusing on the radical magazine *The Masses* and including a full-scale comics treatment of the editors' trial for sedition in 1918.

R.L. Migdal Multimedia's marketing role had been approved in a cabinet meeting chaired by President Wright. The company's initial task had been to create an online gift registry requested by Councilperson Christine Quinn to underpin the New York City Council LGBT Educational Book Drive. The college higher-ups knew they were lucky to get Rebecca as part of the package with me. She was charging a bargain rate. Dean Alvin Reynolds, referring to my planned hundred-hour-a-week schedule, had remarked, "If she doesn't work with you, she'll never see you."

Rebecca had a sharp wit. When I'd introduced her to the staff in April, she'd tried to break the ice with the joke, "Question: Which is worse, working in retail or having a nail hammered through your hand? Answer: How big is the nail?"

They'd every one of them stared at her blankly.

My staff didn't approve of Rebecca's role in the bookstore, but she spent time every week working on her laptop in a back room so we could at least be around each other a bit. Since she'd become a fixture in the store the staff had begun acting coldly polite to her.

I wrote an email back to Vince Tower explaining the merit of each of the Xeroxed images in the packet. He was unmoved and repeated his demand that I remove all the books the staff had cited, plus any other books with possibly objectionable imagery.

I did.

I've returned from Latvia—teaching bookselling for the Soros Foundation—to a family crisis. Two days earlier, eight-year-old Sam had been approached on the street by a man who lived across the way. This guy said Sam had broken the hood ornament off his car. Since Sam had been inside with Chris when the supposed incident occurred, the accusation was absurd. But an hour later, two police officers had knocked on our door and insisted on talking with Sam. They'd pulled Sam outside, onto our porch, and, while one of them blocked Chris in the house, the other had yelled at Sam, "Confess! You know you did it. Tell us the truth! If you don't confess, we're taking you downtown."

Sam was sobbing, and Chris had managed to get past the officer and pull Sam back indoors. The police had left, but sworn they'd be back to arrest Sam.

Now I've gotten back to Chicago and heard this story, I call the Office of Professional Services, to complain. The officer on the phone replies, "This is a big city. Kids his age commit offenses. The officers acted appropriately. They could have taken your kid downtown. How do you know your kid didn't break the hood ornament? Are you taking his word for it?"

The cops don't come back, so I decide we don't have a complaint to pursue.

Years later, I realize that Sam's anxiety problems first appeared around this time.

"Andy!"

I jolted awake. Eight friends were seated in chairs around a curved table facing me. My saxophone was in my lap. Microphones and tape decks filled the room. A broadcast studio inside radio station *WBAI* on the fourteenth floor of a skyscraper on Wall Street. I had fallen asleep in my chair, overworked.

Rebecca said, "Andy, we're talking about our censorship issue being censored in Park Place Bookstore."

We were taping an interview for Ken Gale's *'Nuff Said!* radio show. The editors of *World War 3 Illustrated* were promoting their *Expression! Repression! Revolution!* issue. I myself was only there as saxophone accompanist for editor Seth Tobocman's segment. I had not been expecting to share tales of the conflicts I was navigating as manager of Park Place Bookstore.

"I can't tell that story on the radio."

Seth said, "Come on Andy, they'll never hear it. Besides, you can tell the story—you have the right to." The other editors were looking curious too.

Why was I trying to shield my employees and boss? Was it because I could be fired?

Sure.

Burly bearded radio host Ken Gale interrupted my thoughts, "Well, what is it guys?"

"I can't tell that story."

Ken pressed on with his questions for the editors, and they left me alone.

As I sat in my chair, I felt stupid and cowardly.

"He has power. Look at that: he's controlling us." From behind his desk, the annoyed halfway-house director gestures at twenty-one-year-old Sam, who sits opposite, silent, eyes shut.

Sam is legally independent, so Chris and I hadn't at first been allowed into the office to join this intake interview, during which Sam had spoken not a word.

I object. "You think he's controlling us? That's not fair. He has OCD. He talks politics with me when we're out hiking."

Afterward, Chris, Sam and I agree this residential home— where eight men share two bedrooms—isn't for Sam.

EMAIL SUBJECT: REALIZATION

Hi Sarah,

This morning as I struggled grumpily out of bed to get ready for this job, I reflected on how it was that I applied for and then got this job. I realized that if Sam hadn't died, I definitely would not have applied for this job and they would have hired someone else and the store would still be here and the whole story here would be unfolding differently in some unknown and unknowable way.

I wouldn't have applied for the job because I would have been engaged in Sam's ongoing care, as I had been for twenty-three years.

Part of the reason I did apply for the job was to try jolt myself from my depressed condition, anyway.

So that means the things that happen at Park Place, with me running it, are a direct outcome of Sam's death.

Then I realized, for the first time ever, that Sam foresaw this. He thought about the way his positioning was affecting everyone around him. He had a narrative that visualized his absence from the world. I feel certain of this because everyone does this kind of imagining. And, he was immersing himself in literature about such themes.

I guess the way I stumbled into this thought pattern was because I was remembering how in *War and Peace*, Tolstoy constructs his entire novel around a family with such a situation. Natasha is in love with Andrei, who is doomed. Natasha's brother Nikolai falls in love with Andrei's sister Maria. Both marriages cannot proceed however, since this would set up a situation of cousins being married to cousins. So, there's a period of tension during which Natasha and Nikolai's family, the Rostovs (who were the Tolstoy family—Nikolai is modeled on Leo Tolstoy's father)—have to deal with this question of whether it's Natasha or Nikolai that should be allowed to proceed with their romance.

However, Andrei ends up dying, and this clears the way for Nikolai to marry Maria (and for Leo Tolstoy to be born!)

Andrei therefore is making a sacrifice that enables the entire future to unfold. He's depressed and ended up dead because he kept putting himself in harm's way during the war. He's also always thinking about death.

Anyway, there's an element of this in Sam's death. The way things are unfolding today in my life, with this burst of creativity and challenge that's being pulled out of me by this situation were set in motion by his death. So, his death functions as a sacrifice, ENABLING me to do this.

As with Andrei's death, it's not something anyone involved wanted. Far from it—it's a tragedy. But the essence of tragedy is exactly what is present in Sam's case, because there is a story. I think that a huge part of my mourning has been feeling that his loss is senseless. Of course, I'm an existentialist and absorbed in issues of absurdity and senselessness. But the part of me that's a romantic is always seeking meaning and—well—plot. And Sam's death, when placed in a framework that includes everything that has happened in the past two years, functions in the narrative. It's an explosion that releases pent-up forces. It's a sacrifice, with a redemptive element. Put with extreme oversimplification, he died so the rest of the family could be free to pursue their own lives.

I think this explanation is extremely disturbing, and this is why I haven't been allowing it to surface in my mind. It implies that I might have wanted him to die, which is not true by an infinite degree. I never contemplated his death as a possibility. I was principally concerned that I would die, and he would be left without support—it was always my own death that worried me, relative to him. I never thought he would die.

So, now, this way of thinking about his death—that he was aware of these conditions—that he understood what his death would mean—and that I have made efforts since then to awaken my own potential—helps me to stay focused. I do want to invest his death with meaning. So, I want to be doing what I am doing. I want to save this store.

love, dad

9—A VERY LARGE HOMEWORK ASSIGNMENT: CHAPTER TWO—AN IDEA THAT IN SOME PEOPLE'S MINDS MUST BE CARRIED THROUGH

About two hours later, Jason woke up.

Of course, nobody had noticed that he had been laying on the floor for two hours because his mother was gardening and his father was watching the game, whatever that meant.

When his Dad said that he was going to watch "the game," nobody really knew what it meant, because usually "the game," refers to sports like basketball, football, or sports that that particular person who's saying it, likes to watch. But in Jason's Dad's case, it could mean almost anything. Just a few examples were, tennis, swimming, baseball, hockey, football, ice hockey, basketball, bowling, soccer, volleyball, sports cars, wrestling, running, skiing, Ping-Pong, curling, rugby, boxing, roller-blading, golf, badminton, squash, horse-racing, and even an occasional national miniature golf tournament.

Anyway, when Jason woke up, he realized what he had realized two hours earlier, and got up and groaned.

What was he going to do?

What could he do?

Maybe he could just not do this. After all, what had he done this year?

But then he remembered. His teacher had said that if he didn't get this project done, he would be held back. And that would be genuinely uncool.

In fact, that would be the uncoolest thing that could ever happen to anybody. Only retarded people got held back. Jason M. Zacderard was not a retard.

But he knew all the kids at school would think he was totally stupid if he got held back.

And plus, what would happen in his future life?

He would probably only get into a high school for morons, and a really dumpy college.

And then what would happen if he only got into a high school for morons and a super dumpy college?

He would probably spend the rest of his life in an awful job like McDonald's Worker, or somebody who cleans out toilets.

He must get this done somehow or other.

But it was impossible to write a hundred-page paper honestly in a day. Actually, in about fourteen hours.

So, there was only one thing left to do.

Cheat.

Even though it was immoral, it was better than being a toilet cleaner your whole life.

"Yes," Jason said, "I will do it. It's the only way."

But how was he going to cheat?

He couldn't cheat the traditional way, like you would with a spelling test. It just wouldn't work.

You'd have to cheat in a bizarre way.

A very bizarre way.

But of course, it couldn't be simpler! There were web sites, on the Internet, that you could go onto, and they would do your homework for you, for a price of course.

But that was easy. He had $142.38 up in a box somewhere.

Jason breathed a sigh of relief.

His Dad came in from the living room. "Jason, me and your Mom are going on a date to the movies and a fancy restaurant."

His Mom came in from gardening. "Ready honey?"

"Yep," said his Dad.

"Okay." They walked out the door, and Jason rushed over to the computer.

It was already on. He pressed the little A that represented America Online, and it started up.

Once it had loaded, and the computer said, "You've got mail," he clicked at the top of the screen where you click to write the names of web sites that you want to go to.

"Hmmm. What should I try?" Jason asked himself. "How about, www.homeworkdoers.com?"

He tried it.

Damn, it wasn't a website.

What should he try next?

Of course! www.wedoyourhomeworkforyou.com.

He clicked and the site's first page appeared. "Yes!" he said in an excited kind of voice.

He had found it.

10—DOUBLE CONSCIOUSNESS

They ride through the door in slim umbrella strollers, fancy double-carriages and backpacks. They pull the door open or bounce in on daddy's shoulders. Abandoning their rides in the aisles, they crawl, clamber and climb up the elegant central staircase, clinging to the fancy brass banisters, until they emerge into the second floor. There the colorful puppet stage, painted with beautiful mermaids and a "Yippee Skippy Puppet Theater" marquee, stands on a small black-draped table.

They perch on parents' laps, or take chairs near the front, or gather on pillows and mats with friends and siblings.

I sit facing them, by the stage, a lifetime of musical instruments at my feet. Bansuri flute, chromatic harmonica, Tibetan monk's horn, Thai khaen, South African kalimba, Congolese drum, Japanese shakuhachi, Peruvian ocarina. The troubles of my job are washing away.

I open a window, stick the end of the eight-foot-long monk's horn out, and blow a burst of music down Broadway. I lead the group in shouting, toward the open window, "Announcing the puppet show!"

Shrieks! A monkey is in front of the theater's black curtain! The monkey searches left, right, up, and down, then vanishes.

A blue-cloaked wizard with pointy hat and white beard comes. "Monkey! Monkey!" he calls, then asks the children, "Have you seen my monkey?"

The babies gape, stunned. The toddlers, from their parents' laps, point, straining forward. School-age children shout, "He went that way!"

"This way?" the wizard asks, exiting left.

The monkey enters right, and, as the children scream, dances up and down, examines the stage margins left and right, then once again exits left. Some children call, "The wizard is looking for you," but the monkey must not have heard.

The wizard enters right, searches up and down, left and right, then finally, in response to the many informative voices, asks, "What? What did you say? You saw my monkey? Where?"

The monkey pokes his head from behind the worried wizard, then vanishes.

The monkey swings from above as the wizard pokes out from the theatre searching downward among the children.

I'm playing all my musical instruments—one after the other or several at once—providing riffs and accents, boops, and beeps. I love accompanying Rebecca.

After a few minutes, the wizard finds the monkey, they hug, and I address the fifty-odd attendees. "Welcome to Park Place Bookstore. My name is Andy, and this is Fractured Fables, by the Yippee Skippy Puppet Theater. Who would like to pick a story from the bucket?" I point to a child, ask their name, and hold the bucket toward them.

"Oh, you picked two by accident? All right, our first story will be *Little Red Riding Hood* meets *Three Billy Goats Gruff!*"

So begins an hour of interactive, improvised comedy featuring a cast of dozens of puppet characters, inverting well-known plots, screwing up old-fashioned morals, lobbing topical political satire over the heads of the kids at the delighted parents, and singing weird versions of familiar songs. (Shark MacDonald tries to eat each animal on his farm but gets stomped by a bunny.) The puppets request advice from the children and accept it strangely. The little pig's house should be made of what? Straw? The pig drinks cans of soda and builds a house of drinking straws. Of course, no props, only characters—but the children see the scene clearly.

Some kids are fervent fans who drag their parents to us every weekend. These parents tell us of their children presenting puppet shows at home. Some parents are Broadway actors, choreographers, concert musicians, TV stars. Parents comment, of Rebecca, "I forgot there was only one person back there!" Of their two-year-old daughters, "She never sat through something this long before." Of their sons, "I never saw him so engaged."

Around midnight, Sarah and I arrive at the Amherst house, from Logan Airport. After her junior year in Florence, Sarah is moving to Brooklyn for the summer—she has an apartment lined up—but first she's spending a few days at home.

Chris is away at a meditation retreat. Rebecca has gotten dinner ready.

Twenty-three-year-old Sam had to move back home last summer, after his liver's adverse reaction to Clozaril ended his year of independence in the Northampton apartment. These days, he never eats with others, but as we prepare to gather around the pasta and salad, I poke my head into his room. "Sarah's back! Come and read?"

He's been reading aloud to me for hours each night: last week, One Hundred Years of Solitude, *this week,* The Count of Monte Cristo. *He comes to the kitchen and smiles sideways. Sarah goes over to hug him.*

He joins us at the table, and—as Sarah, Rebecca and I eat—Sam reads in a firm and dramatic voice from the chapter where Franz and Albert, kidnapped and taken to a bandit hideout, encounter the notorious Luigi Vampa, a startlingly cultured fellow who's calmly perusing Caesar's Commentaries.

The puppets were stars among the young *Fractured Fables* faithful, but when Julie Andrews came to Park Place, I was the starstruck one.

She'd been my first screen idol. I was six years old, at my big sister's birthday party in 1966. Nancy's girlfriends and I ate dinner and cake, then piled into station wagons and drove to the theater. *Mary Poppins* left me exhausted with pleasure. I fell asleep in the car coming back, crammed in with the other children.

The next year too on Nancy's birthday it was dinner, cake and—this time—*The Sound of Music*. What a treat: Julie Andrews again; the crowded theater; swept away.

Then, decades later, when Sam and Sarah were little, the *Mary Poppins* videotape had been a very frequent rental.

In September of 2012, publicist Melanie Chang of Little, Brown emailed to ask if Park Place Bookstore would host Julie Andrews, who was seventy-five and artistically active—writing and directing. She'd published twenty children's books: this time it was *Julie Andrews' Treasury for all Seasons: Poems and Songs to Celebrate the Year.* This opportunity came in the midst of a staffing meltdown—two more full-timers had quit— but Sarah put out a call among her friends for help.

The black Range Rover pulled up to the side entrance and out came the managers and Julie Andrews. I whisked her in, and she had to climb those long, steep back stairs. In through the security door, the warehouse hallway, and the only office that we'd been able to make bright and tidy. On a table, we had flowers, fruit, a pitcher of ice water, and the requested tea.

About half of the room, however, was a mountain of lumpy white-sheet-covered something. Don't look at that.

Julie Andrews was warm and charming. She paid attention to everyone. We were smitten.

After a few minutes chatting, we asked her to exit the office across the sales floor, to the blocked-off region we'd created by pushing the rolling bookcases to make an isolated quadrant, as requested in her list of ground-rules. She'd be seated within the hidden area. Only at the beginning of each person's encounter would they catch sight of her. Everyone would get a private fifteen seconds.

But she refused. Instead, she wished to exit through the other door, go into our back hallway, and peek into our other rooms.

The warehouse area was a wreck. The store had been running with less staffing than usual for months. I would have preferred that Julie Andrews of all people not look back there, but it was too late.

She peeked into the messy rooms and smiled conspiratorially, saying, "I always like to look in the back."

She emerged, and the customers at the top of the stairway greeted her. As we escorted her across to the autographing alcove, she waved, and sweetly said, "Hello."

Throughout this two-hour, hushed program, the customers were patient and reverential. Many, like myself, were dealing with the vivid re-experiencing of lost magic. I did know she'd had a fifty-year career since my childhood—twenty since my children's—but she rendered me a happy kid. If she'd tired of having this effect on people, she was good at concealing it. Parents and children emerged glowing from their fifteen seconds in her presence.

*   *   *

SON OF REBEL BOOKSELLER

Thirteen-year-old Sam has spent much of the summer inside at the computer, immersed in Age of Empires, *a real-time-strategy game. We try to come up with ways to get him off the machine. Since he loves movies, we arrange for our indie-filmmaker friend John Cannon to provide movie-making lessons twice a week.*

Sam likes doing special effects. He develops a sci-fi comedy script. He and John produce the film; family and friends are drafted to play parts.

BABY F. HUEY AND THE WORLD—SCENE TWO

PETER: Well, I guess The Big Switcheroony should be up around somewhere. Oh, here it is.

Big room. The Big Switcheroony [a mechanical switch] is at the end of it, and, between it and Peter, is a person: The Guarder of The Big Switcheroony. My dad Andy should play this part.

THE GUARDER OF THE BIG SWITCHEROONY: *(Snores).*

Peter tiptoes past The Guarder of The Big Switcheroony. Peter almost pulls The Big Switcheroony, but then, The Guarder of The Big Switcheroony wakes up.

THE GUARDER OF THE BIG SWITCHEROONY: Wait! I will make you stop! I have special powers! I will make you turn into a little ball of whipped cream! MA-CA-NA-VICH-CA-PUFFF!

The Guarder of The Big Switcheroony turns into a little ball of whipped cream.

PETER: *(Pulls The Big Switcheroony)* Well that was nice and fast!

*　　*　　*

By the way, what was that mountain of lumpy stuff covered by white sheets, in the back office?

Two hundred unopened boxes of newly released books.

They'd been ordered between April and August, during meetings with publishers' sales representatives. On arrival, union receiving clerk and shop steward Phil Marciano had refused to enter their data into our computer inventory system. In my opinion, he had plenty of time in his day to do this. But Phil pointed out that new-title data entry was not in his job description. At Park Place Bookstore, the buyer was the person who was supposed to do this task, not the receiving clerk. That buyer was me.

I was so short-staffed that I was always on the sales floor. I did not have time to deal with this data entry stuff, so, I was ignoring those boxes.

Phil wasn't. More were arriving every day. Phil was upset because he was also in charge of opening the mail, and he knew that bills for those unopened boxes were piling up, not being submitted to the business office. Soon, those unsubmitted bills for those unopened boxes would come due for payment. If the bills weren't paid, the vendors could put the store on credit hold.

Phil began to take photographs of the piles of boxes each day. He emailed the photos to Vince Tower.

I was summoned to a formal meeting with Vince Tower and Norma Rendell. I was told that I would be fired in six weeks, if in that time I had not caught up on the receiving backlog. Also, I was to hire an assistant manager.

I lost my temper and started shouting.

No, I had not replaced Zack, Irene, and Lucy, the full-timers who'd quit! I was working flat out—a hundred hours a week—to keep critical functions going, and sales were great!

As I'd suspected, consumer demand was the real driver of our business, not our vaunted expert staff! We were in one of the wealthiest, most highly educated, most densely populated neighborhoods on the planet! We had a huge selection of terrific children's books and toys and our book-loving Upper West Side customers were capable of self-service!

Myra's strategy had been to maintain over-large teams of expert booksellers to jawbone customers, and the resulting purchases hadn't been subsidizing this fabulous offering! The math was simple: we weren't selling diamonds! For years, Park Place Bookstore's average cash register transaction had been under thirty dollars!

I was running a successful business turnaround by reducing payroll! On a week to week basis the store was breaking even!

Hello! I was hired with explicit instructions from President Wright to cut the deficit!

For God's sake, I was told I would get a bonus of five thousand dollars if I could cut the loss in half, and by shedding half my inherited staff, I had done even better!

Admittedly—I had made an error, ordering new titles in such quantity. I had been following Myra's approach of stocking new publications very broadly. I was now convinced the store didn't need to test so many new titles. Most of our sales came from older titles, which were a better bet to sell, and operationally inexpensive to replenish.

But the fact that Phil's union job description didn't include new-title data entry—a task moderately common among workers with his job in other stores—was the real problem! He was playing an "I cannot" game of chicken with me!

Norma sat silent.

Vince was unimpressed: the books were piled up in the back office. Because of his job description, Phil could not enter the data. To begin with, the assistant manager. Then, I had to hire help to catch up on data entry. I could hire temporary workers, since this task was not in any union job description.

    Six weeks. Fired. Final warning.

    Well—what I hadn't been told: a contract negotiation was in progress. The Service Workers International Union was insisting that headcount in the bookstore be maintained. Otherwise, staff were overworked, and therefore underpaid.

"Sam, what's the plan?"

Twenty-one-year old Sam leaps up the steps, fumbles with his key, unlocks his apartment, and rushes in.

I follow. "We have to talk—"

He slams his bedroom door. I grasp the doorknob, but it won't turn. He must be holding it from the inside.

"We can figure this out!"

He won't let the knob turn.

I back into the living room, talking at his door. "We can make a new plan. Things will work out. We'll talk tomorrow, okay?"

What can I do? I leave.

I left the meeting with Vince and Norma, in shock.

    Running the bookstore would be less work for me if I hired more staff, but President Wright had signaled clearly that to keep the store from being closed I needed to cut costs. Now Vince's decisions would prevent me.

    By hiring, I'd benefit personally in the short term, but be penalized long term.

    I began to develop a double consciousness. I wanted to save money: I was proud of my proven skill at running a store for profitability. But Vince Tower's refusal to permit me to run a profitable store meant I shouldn't focus on running a profitable store.

I decided I no longer cared about the current year's deficit. My goal had always been larger anyway: to somehow rescue the bookstore. The labor union was successfully competing for the funds in my budget, but I resolved not to let this keep me from seeking in-store and online sales growth through R.L. Migdal Multimedia's marketing outreach and website development.

Eleven-year-old Sam takes a poetry class at the School of the Art Institute; his poem is printed in the group's anthology.

RESCUE

A cow, a cow, a wonderful cow
Looked pale, in a dungeon,
With chains galore—
And I jumped in the cell
Where the cow lay strangling,
And I loosed his chains galore—
And his face was as round
As a cookie from joy!
And we escaped together
And were very happy.

Ever since I'd come to Park Place Bookstore young people had been dropping off their resumes. Within a few weeks, I'd hired Heidi French as assistant manager and Robert Mandala as temporary full-timer doing data entry. The store was caught up opening all those boxes within six weeks. We were back to losing money.

11—A VERY LARGE HOMEWORK ASSIGNMENT: CHAPTER THREE—THE WEB SITE'S FRONT PAGE

The website appeared. It was white and it had an introduction at the top of it that went down until the middle of the page. Then was the section that said, "Our Mission."

Jason first read the introduction. It went like this:

At www.wedoyourhomeworkforyou.com, we have a full-time 24-hour staff always ready to help you with your homework needs. We can write any kind of report, from a one-and-a-half-page second-grade report about what fish are, to a fifty-five-page tenth-grade report about Encyclopedia Brown-books, to a sixth-grade science-fair project, to anything imaginable.

Our specialized writers can write in a third-graders' writing, or an eleventh-graders' writing, or anybody's, for God's sakes!

We have also won the Best Homework Doers' Web Award.

Then at the bottom of the page, it said:

<u>Our Mission</u>
We know the plight of children young and old. How they are tortured by intolerable homework that teachers that can only be explained as evil give them! Our mission is to rid the country of torture-houses known more commonly and incorrectly as schools.

So, part of what you spend here will be donated to an organization that's first and only priority is getting rid of schools.

They do this not by lobbying the Senate, or by blowing up the places of torture themselves. They do this by sneaking into the schools and messing up their computers, so it says the school owes a huge amount, when in fact it does not owe a dime.

Then the organization sends bills for things the school never bought. As the school gets poorer and poorer from these debts, the organization starts mailing the school letters saying that there is a huge business in selling used couches, and that the school's only chance of making money is by allowing couches to be sold in certain rooms of the school.

They will have already tripled the tuition, cut the teachers' paychecks in half, and used so much paper in applying for grants that the T.S.S.—or Tree-Saving Society—will have sent numerous nasty letters to the school. All this fails because of the rising bills. The school will be forced to start selling couches in small numbers of rooms at first. But then, more and more, if they stopped, they'd go out of business for sure. Then they have to cut classes because they need more couch-selling space.

This will continue until finally the whole school's only preoccupation will be selling couches. Then it will not be a school. It will be a couch liquidation facility.

Only when all the schools in the country are like this will we be satisfied.

12—A VERY LARGE HOMEWORK ASSIGNMENT: CHAPTER FOUR—$5,000 DISCOVERED AND RELUCTANTLY USED

After reading all this, Jason felt terrific. It made him tingle all over to know that by the time he reached ninth grade in school there would be no school to go to, just a couch liquidation facility.

The web site's first page continued. There were twelve highlighted things to click on. If you were a first grader, you would click on the button that said, "Grade 1." If you were a second grader, you would press "Grade 2." And so on.

Jason clicked "Grade 7."

Another page appeared. There were several places to click on this one also. There was a button that said, "0-3 pages," "4-7 pages," "8-15," "16-35," "36-60," and "Science Fairs." He clicked the "More Than 60 Pages" icon.

A recorded message said, "If you are not fooling around and really have a report over 60 pages long, please hold." Jason did so. What else was there to do?

After about a minute, the recorded message came back. "The person who you will hear next will be an employee of www.wedoyourhomeworkforyou.com."

About ten seconds later, the screen changed from a web site image to a man, sitting behind a desk, in the middle of a very large and very busy room, with lots of desks and lots of people frantically running back and forth, giving other people papers and talking on cell phones.

The man Jason was looking at was about forty-five, and had brown hair, with a big bald spot in the center of his head.

"All right, let's see," he exclaimed, in a true Chicago accent. "You're a seventh grader who needs to have a report over sixty pages done. Don't see many of those." He talked fast. "All right, so when do you need this done?"

Jason stuttered, "Well, sort of, really soon."

"What's really soon mean? I gotta know," exclaimed the man behind the desk.

"Well, well," Jason stuttered. "Tomorrow," he blurted out.

"TOMORROW!" the man screamed. His face almost jumped out of his head. "Whaddya mean by that!" the man was screaming. "You want a sixty-page report done by tomorrow?!"

"Actually, it's supposed to be a hundred pages," Jason said meekly.

"Oh God, I just hope I don't get assigned it," the man said. "But, do you have any idea how much a hundred-page report costs, if it's going to be done tomorrow morning? Let's see exactly how much it would cost—uh, uh, ahh," the man hummed. "Here we go. For overnight service of anything longer than sixty pages, it costs—oh my good Lord," he gulped, "it costs, it costs, $50 a page for overnight service. And $50 a page for 100 pages is $5,000."

"Oh, God!" Jason moaned. *How the heck was he supposed to get that kind of money?*

"One good thing though is that the cost includes tax."

"Oh great," Jason moaned, "Could you please hold on, I'll be right back."

"All right," the man said, as if the man thought it would be a long time before Jason came back.

Jason slowly got out of the chair in which he had been seated for the last two hours or so and walked over toward the stairs, and went up them, and went up to his room.

What was he going to do?

He had to have this done, but how the heck was he going to get $5,000?

He couldn't, that's all there was when he came right down to it. He just couldn't.

And then he would get held back and everyone at school would think he was stupid.

No, he would be stupid.

And for the rest of his life, whenever he applied for a job, or whenever he tried to get into a college, they would look at his resume and say, "Hmmm. Looks good. Looks good. Oh, he got held back. He's 'special.' We can't accept him."

Jason started crying, and then sobbing. What would he do the rest of his life?

Oh yeah, he remembered from when he was thinking about this before. He would be a toilet cleaner. Maybe he could promote to a urinal cleaner.

Oh, what was going to happen to him? Oh, oh, oh!

Then he realized that there was something he could do. But it would be so immoral!

He remembered that his parents had just gotten two new credit cards, and he remembered they had exactly $2,500 on each of them.

No, he couldn't do that. What would his parents do?

It's true they'd probably never suspect him. But if they suddenly lost $5,000, wouldn't that hurt them?

But then, on the other side, there was the toilet cleaner idea.

Well, this was a tough one, but he'd take the credit cards.

He got up from his chair, in his room, and went over to his parents' room. They always kept their credit cards on their top shelf, and not in their wallet, because the credit cards were just for safety. Jason's parents never planned to use them.

He reluctantly went into their room and over to the top shelf, and slowly reached for the credit cards and pulled them off the shelf.

Sighing, he walked downstairs.

The man on the screen of the computer was still there. "Where the heck you been, I almost hanged up!"

Jason sat down at the computer again. "I have the money." He waved the credit cards.

"All $5,000 of it?"

"All $5,000 of it." He paused. "I'm using credit cards. There's two of them."

"Great," the man said, rubbing his bald spot. "By the way, what's this report on?"

Jason sighed again. "It's called 'The Detailed Study of Cultures, Migrations and Civilizations of the Last Ten Thousand Years.'"

"Oh!" He paused, shocked. "All right. Any specifications?"

"No."

"OK. I'll need your credit card numbers."

"Ugh," Jason moaned. He knew he had to do it. So, he did it in a burst, in one movement. "6-5-4-3-8-9-1-4-6-8-9-3, and 9-1-8-4-7-6-5-3-2-6-7-1."

"OK, great, it will be done tomorrow morning at six-thirty AM. See you then."

Jason sighed, and signed off America Online, the Internet, and shut down his computer.

SON OF REBEL BOOKSELLER

13—I WON'T BET MY SOUL TO THE DEVIL

MONDAY, MARCH 11, 2013

Chimes; six-twenty-five; snooze.
    Chimes; six-thirty-five; snooze.
    Chimes; six-forty-five; snooze.
    Chimes; six fifty-five; end. I lurched sideways, my hip aching, wrapped myself in a towel from the bedpost, stumbled to the shower, woke up in the hot water, washed my hair, dried, pulled on yesterday's corduroy pants and a fresh shirt. Bailey the poodle needed my boost into bed. I kissed Rebecca.
    It was Sam's birthday. He was twenty-six. Would have been. Was.
    My hip-pain asserted itself and I took some Ibuprofen from the bedside bottle, got water, limped downstairs, then out the door. *The New York Times* was on the front step and I tucked it under my arm as I walked downhill on Cannon Place around the corner onto 238th Street. I was struggling to move fast because I'd overslept. Should be nine minutes to the station.
    It was a mild, late winter day. I hobbled above the Major Deegan Expressway, past Bronx Alehouse—our late night local—up to Broadway. In some agony, I climbed the steps to the elevated platform.
    The one-train was pulling in. I'd extricated my wallet, and the Metrocard. I swiped it—nothing—swiped it again—nothing—a third time worked, and I plowed through the

turnstile, ran along the train, as it slowed, to a farther car with maybe a seat. I pushed in, jamming myself between other riders, at the last minute grabbing my right foot, twisting it under my right buttock and settling on top. It was the least painful way to ride. As my aching muscles stretched, I relaxed. I would not be late to open the store.

I squeezed my iPhone from my pocket and checked for emails. For weeks, I'd been using a rapid response tactic. Whenever I saw one of my new best friend's critical emails—which were usually addressed to Vince Tower with me copied—I rebutted immediately.

Jan Smart had quit in December to become Director of Children's Literature at Conquest Academies: she was teaching teachers about the books she'd helped select for their classrooms. Vince Tower had named my new best friend to run Bulk Orders; my new best friend had spent the past ten weeks hounding me.

My best friend's pet peeve was unpaid bills. Park Place College was a fifty-million-dollar-a-year non-profit, and the bookstore was a small piece of that. There were cycles and crunches around various college divisions in different seasons. Sometimes the business office didn't cut checks for our vendors as promptly as we'd have liked. This performance wasn't good enough for my new best friend.

There were no emails from my friend so far. As the one-train rumbled toward Manhattan, I slipped *The New York Times* from its blue plastic sleeve. In Rome, the cardinals were electing a Pope. I thought, "Sam would have loved that."

When he was in middle school, Sam—such a history buff—had become knowledgeable about the expansion of electoral democracy. The fact that the Catholic Church was having a democratic election would have struck him as funny.

The one-train went underground, surfaced at 125th Street, and descended again. At the 110th Street stop, I launched off my foot and limped out of the train onto the platform. It was seven-fifty-six.

I grabbed the handrail and hoisted myself up the stairs to Broadway. One block north, I entered Samad's and, from the cooler, grabbed a plain yogurt and a plastic cup of fresh-squeezed orange juice—no time for green tea. I paid, accepted the paper bag, and went two doors north to our building's side entrance. I punched the code, listened for the click, pulled the heavy door, and forced myself up the steep stairs, thinking about Julie Andrews.

She'd returned to our store just last month on a book tour supporting *The Very Fairy Princess Follows Her Heart*, this time accompanied by her daughter, co-author Emma Walton Hamilton. When I'd greeted them at the side door, Julie Andrews had said, "Oh I remember these stairs. Last fall, I looked up and thought 'I don't know how I will do this.'"

I'd expressed surprise, and she'd explained, "I've had ankle replacement since I saw you last." I'd felt terrible: there was an elevator on the 112th Street side.

But I got her failure to complain. I'd been refusing to notice my own body's signals. Last week, I'd finally seen a doctor. She'd x-rayed my hip and told me it was arthritis: I should keep off my feet. Not helpful. She'd been more worried about my heart murmur—mitral valve prolapse—which I regarded as background noise. I even had a nickname for my heart when I was short of breath: Old Thump-Bump.

Also, still grieving after two years counted as clinical depression. I needed therapy. Yes. No. The fear of unfurling the story to a stranger. I'd emailed Sarah; she'd answered, "Obviously therapy sounds like a good idea and something we should all be doing." Braver than me.

* * *

After our visit with silent, twenty-year-old Sam in the locked mental-health ward, Chris and I meet with his social worker. Five minutes in, she begins to berate us. "Of course, he knows something's wrong. Your secrecy is making it worse. You have to tell him." We give in. She'll set up a meeting; we'll tell him about our planned divorce. He'll get a shot of Ativan first; perhaps this will permit him to respond.

Next day, in a darkened office, the social worker asks Sam, "Do you know why we're all here?"

"You read my journal, but that was just a story. I'm not going to commit suicide—it was something I wrote to see what it was like to think about."

Social worker and doctor exchange glances. They had not expected the shot of Ativan to reveal this—which none of us had known of.

"It's all right, we understand you aren't planning to commit suicide. Thank you for setting our minds at ease."

The nurse escorts him out. Our divorce is still a secret.

Up on the second floor I punched another code and opened the door to the warehouse. I moved down the hall, used a key to unlock back rooms, hung up my coat, studied the chart on the door to remind myself which staff were scheduled, then used a different key to unlock the door to the sales floor.

Sixty seconds to disarm. As the system beeped, I limped toward the stairs, swerving to hit light-switches as I went, then descended to street level.

Electrodes leap free, releasing rapid beeps. I run for help. A nurse comes and shows me how to restick each unstuck node. Every moment, gasp, gasp—my minute child in his fish-tank—gasp, then a wire jumps off his side—beep, beep, beep—he jerks as I retape the electrode to his skin. Surrounding us dozens of other babies are unattended in their tanks. Some are startlingly tiny and very still, others writhe and cast off their wires, filling the full-lit room with sharp beeping. With so few nurses and so many babies, the chorus of beeps is varied and shifting, but uninterrupted. Sometimes it's my baby—I fail to retape—I run to find the nurse for help. He has fresh tape, reattaching the wire.

Where are the other parents? Have some babies been here hours, or days? When can my baby leave?

I moved around behind the t-shirt rack and through the door into the little room under the stairwell. At the keypad, I punched another code. The beeping stopped.

I held down the red button, raising the grate guarding our 112th Street plate glass window. I flipped more light switches. I came from under the stairs and went to a keyhole near the front, where I inserted a key, then turned it to raise another grate—the one guarding our window on Broadway.

I switched on more lights. I unlocked the front door and set the special-events sandwich board that Rebecca had chalked yesterday out on the sidewalk. We had a great week of programs coming up—including a Teddy Bear Clinic to help kids become comfortable with hospital visits, presented by Park Place students from the Child Life program, plus another in the *Save the Planet Brigade* environmental education series, and more concerts with guitarist Danna Banana. I came back inside, went behind the counter, turned on the computers and logged in.

I needed to pee, and I remembered that I couldn't do this easily—it would involve climbing the stairs up to our building's third floor restrooms or going next door to the college. This was because the bookstore's toilet was out of order. I needed to do another round of complaining. For an entire week, we had not been able to use our toilet because the college maintenance people were stalemated with the building super about who should pay the plumber. Meanwhile, customers had to hold it, and often so did I.

I looked at the stack of paperwork I'd left next to the cash register. Last night—Sunday—besides the usual invoice cover sheets, I'd organized the dozens of monthly vendor statements for analysis. My new best friend's emailed complaints had roused Vince Tower to the point that Vince had last Friday sent an email explicitly directing me to carry out this analysis. I didn't want to, because I didn't have password access to the business office's accounting system, so there was no way for me to see what bills were already posted. I suspected they all were, but I couldn't prove it.

My friend was asserting that Bulk Orders wouldn't be able to order the thousands of dollars of toys needed by Conquest Academies for their "incentives" program until all our vendor statements, with their hundreds of line items, had been analyzed—by me personally—to guarantee no vendor had cause to put us on credit hold. If we were put on hold and failed to get our toys on time, Bulk Orders would miss a deadline, and we might lose the Conquest account.

I'd been considering an alternative. Now, standing there, I decided to go ahead and do the exact thing Myra Raines had warned me never to do. I would give my vendor statements to Ron Turbide in the business office.

I knew Ron could analyze them since he had access to the accounting system. I did not know why Myra had said I should never give vendor statements to Ron.

My best friend—who'd worked at Park Place for years—had mentioned that Mariela Juarez was hired only a year before me. It was to Mariela that I'd been told to give invoices.

I'd had very little interaction with Ron Turbide. I didn't know his job title, but his cubicle was near Mariela's—maybe he was her supervisor? Now that Vince Tower had been swayed by my new best friend into joining what felt like an irrational assault, I needed someone else on my side. Last Friday, I'd asked Ron if he'd like to analyze our vendor statements. He'd said yes, seeming pleased.

Phil Marciano walked in the front door. He and I had reached a détente since last fall: I'd hired three part-timers to help with receiving and data entry. I asked, "Okay if you stand at the register while I run to the business office?"

"You know I can't ring."

"Yeah, but it's dead so far."

I was relieved I'd be able to hand off the statements before any of my new best friend's emails hit Vince. Also, I could pee at the college. As I darted out the door, though, I remembered the business office wouldn't open till nine. I came back in, and Phil went upstairs to his receiving desk in our large back room. I took a breath, perched on the high stool at the counter, and tried to attend to my yogurt and juice.

It's hot. Sam, aged two-and-a-half, is on my shoulders. We're climbing the mountain road above Heredia, Costa Rica. A wrinkled man emerges from his house with a tiny cup. He hands the strawberry juice over my head. Sam grasps the luscious gift, then—tips the cup over. The pink juice cascades. The kind man's smile does not waver. "Le gusta ver el agua corrir," he says.

I had a customer, but the cash register wasn't working. I realized my log-in to the IBID point of sale system hadn't succeeded. I didn't want to make the customer wait, so I conducted her sale manually, collecting data for later input. A second customer had to be handled this way too.

I rebooted the machine, but this didn't help. Since our computers ran on servers housed in the college next door, I was often impotent during such tech crises. I phoned the college help desk and left a message begging for assistance.

I heard a tapping on the outside of the Broadway display window and glanced behind myself. It was Jenny Sheridan, in a bike helmet. I went around from the cash desk to the front door and held it open as she wheeled in her bike.

"Can it be here?" she asked, leaning it against the inside of the 112th Street window.

"The strollers will block it in at storytime," I answered, "But maybe we'll be done by ten-thirty?"

"Sure, it's just the summer list."

Jenny was the HarperCollins sales representative. Her territory was huge—extending to Minneapolis—but she lived a few blocks from Park Place Bookstore. I knew she'd packed her kids off to school and zipped over for this appointment.

Ellen Shaw had arrived for her nine o'clock shift, and took over at the register, which was working—the help desk people must have restarted our server. Jenny and I went upstairs to the special orders counter, where we could have our meeting while I monitored the second-floor sales area.

Like me, Jenny had spent her early years working in several Chicago bookstores—in her case, Women & Children First and then Unabridged Bookstore. We'd known of each other, but never met, so Park Place Bookstore had been the first time we'd worked together. One of the things I liked most about buying from Jenny was that it reminded me of my younger days. Now, after all the turmoil in the book industry, we were both still in the business. The good fight.

* * *

Six indie bookstores working together have pulled off our blockbuster It Takes a Village *book release at Chicago Theater. Now, author Hillary Clinton has spent the past half-hour shaking hands with a thousand attendees. Eight-year-old Sam and seven-year-old Sarah have waited so patiently. At last, it's their turns. Hillary shakes their hands, saying, "I like your tie! I like your dress!"*

I got myself set up in my database to place the order, but Jenny was having a problem with her laptop. As she rebooted, I stepped away to set up the chairs for the storyhour.

We held these upstairs, in the central sales area. I rolled several stacks of chairs from the aisle near the exit by the elevator and set them up in five rows of six.

Jenny was ready. As I scrolled through the HarperCollins title display, Jenny pitched in a concise, pithy way—mixing personal and industry considerations. I rapidly chose how many copies I needed, and then she pitched the next book.

As we worked, the ten o'clock crew was arriving, slipping past into the large back room to hang up their coats. Asha Phillips, who'd previously worked at New York Public Library; Alva Rogers, playwright, actress and arts educator; Margaret Croft, who'd worked for me at Eric Carle Museum Bookstore; and Dara Andante—a full-timer who'd worked for Park Place Bookstore twelve years, and before that at Barnes & Noble.

It was nearing ten-thirty. Jenny had pushed us through a pretty large list after all, and the order was finished. We headed downstairs, and she extricated her bike from the buildup of baby-strollers.

I moved through the picture book section choosing the books I'd use for storyhour. I went back upstairs, set my stack of books onto the plush red swivel chair at the front of the storytelling area, and then—as the parents, nannies, and grandparents, babies, toddlers and preschoolers emerged from the stairwell and settled onto mats and into chairs—I darted away, down the back hallway, through the security door, and up the stairs to the building's third floor.

My hip always loosened up once the day was happening. Maybe the adrenaline helped. I zipped down the hall to the men's room, punched in the access code, went in and peed, washed my hands, ran back down the hall, down the stairs, punched the code to get back into our store, came down our warehouse hall, out past the special orders desk where Jenny and I had just spent the past ninety minutes, and onto the sales floor where forty kids and adults awaited storytime.

I started by playing kalimba, then said, "Welcome to storyhour. This is Park Place Bookstore—babies, if you don't know, that's where you are. I'm Andy."

We started with Raffi's *Spider on the Floor,* which I performed in a way that encouraged adults to tickle their kids.

Next, I read Byron Barton's *Dinosaurs, Dinosaurs*, with which I requested the group join in by rasping the word "dinosaurs" every time it recurred.

I vocalized slowly and musically, keeping eye contact with the children, shifting my focus, making sure I looked directly in each child's eyes many times during the performance, smiling specially at each, recognizing each for her effort to contribute to the sonic environment. I interspersed friendly asides to the adults about the activity of their children.

The third piece was the Robert Louis Stevenson poem, "Windy Nights," from *A Child's Garden of Verses.* I used the Tasha Tudor illustrated version, and I prefaced the performance for the adults by alerting them that the man who wrote this classic children's poetry collection was the same who wrote *Dr Jekyll and Mr Hyde,* and *Treasure Island.* I told the children a horse would be galloping, and I encouraged the toddlers to stamp, and the parents to bounce babies on their laps. I kept the rhythm with my feet and legs while chanting the iambs forcefully. I performed the poem twice. It left me breathless and in some leg pain.

As often happened during storyhour, I was seeing and hearing my preschoolers Sam and Sarah in the kids present. A traumatic, addictive experience.

I'm driving the family van when from the back I hear five-year-old Sam and three-year-old Sarah having this unlikely conversation with their five-year-old friend Michael:

MICHAEL: When you die, you go to heaven with the angels.

SAM: When you die, you go to nature with the flowers and trees.

SARAH: When you die, you get born again in a baby.

I'm delighted with their profound yet calm assertions, which make death sound like an adventure.

I asked the children what their favorite kind of taco was, and after we pretended to eat those, I performed Adam Rubin's *Dragons Love Tacos*. I stopped mid-book and requested advice about whether it was wise to turn the page that would reveal the fiery destruction of the hero's house. The children insisted, but I resisted, before finally giving in and discovering that lurid catastrophe. We screamed for a while.

I finished with *Little Blue Truck Leads the Way,* another piece I performed while keeping a beat stamping my legs. This book always made me think of its friendly, understated author Alice Schertle, who'd come so regularly to the exhibition openings at Eric Carle Museum. Her success with the *Little*

Blue Truck franchise had come late in her career as a poet, which I felt was a lovely thing.

That was forty minutes. I reviewed which books we'd just read, thanked everyone for coming, and reminded them that we had free storyhours at ten-thirty, seven days a week, and free puppet shows on Saturdays and Sundays at one. Then I retreated to our large back room, where Phil was receiving books.

He handed me the phone. The caller was an official from the Occupational Safety and Health Administration: OSHA. An anonymous complaint had been telephoned in from an employee of Park Place Bookstore. This person had stated there was no toilet available for him, which violated the law.

I told this guy from OSHA the complaint was not true. Yes, the bookstore's own toilet had been out of order for a week, but there were men's and women's bathrooms with multiple stalls inside our building, one floor up. Our staff had been using these all week.

The man from OSHA asked why I thought this complaint had been lodged. I told him someone was hassling me. He seemed sympathetic, but said I'd need to write a letter, on letterhead, stating the truth of the matter, and fax it to him.

I spent the next ten minutes performing this task.

Finally, I had my moment to run paperwork over to the business office. I headed downstairs, alerting Dara Andante—the senior union bookseller—that I'd be out of the store for fifteen minutes. I grabbed my stack of invoices and vendor statements. I went out the door onto Broadway, turned left onto 112th Street, and ran two doors down to the wide orange awning over the front entrance to Park Place College. I pulled the tall glass door open by its stainless-steel pole-handle, entered the foyer, pulled the second glass door open, and was in the lobby. I fished in my pocket for my wallet, extracted my magnetic ID card and waved it over the bar-code reader, causing the turnstile to open. I passed through. Since it was late morning, the lobby—with its tree in the central atrium surrounded by quadrants of couch seating—was empty. I waved to Roger at the security desk and he smiled. I swerved left to the elevators, punched the button, and waited. The elevator doors opened, I entered and hit seven.

Child's Play is on tour for the week; I'm calling from a hotel in downstate Illinois. Chris says she's had a phone conversation with my sister Nancy, and they've decided on a two-year plan to have children. Each of them will have a baby in two years.

I'm unprepared.

We're actively searching for a location for the bookstore we're going to launch. I'm working fulltime as a touring children's theater actor. She has part-time bookstore jobs at Guild, Rizzoli, and Seminary Co-op. The practical reasons not to have a baby are obvious.

More important, it is one of the bases of our relationship that we both agree that it is a bad thing for people to bring a child into this world only to suffer and see suffering.

And what right does my sister have to get my girlfriend to want a baby?

How could such a conversation have happened?

What about me? Am I not involved in this huge decision that affects my life as well?

I do not express these thoughts. I say it's okay with me. What else can I say? It seems to be a decision without meaning. Can you really choose the birth of another person? Does one person "have" another?

A few days later I'm back in Chicago. I take the bus from Victor and June's house to Clark Street and walk to a bar where Chris has suggested we meet to discuss her and Nancy's two-year-plan.

I sit at a table that's high. My feet dangle from the bar stool. As I contemplate having a child, I feel the world falling away from me, my feet not touching the ground, the world not a place I know.

I left the elevator and went down the hallway.

Hushed anxiety was always the dominant mood in the business office. Every conversation felt shadowed by the possible criticism of auditors.

In the main room were nine cubicles. I knew the names of half the people, and I knew the kinds of paperwork I needed to periodically submit to three of them. Now I brought my invoices to Mariela's counter. It was covered with stacks of similar paperwork from other college divisions. I recognized invoices I'd submitted the previous week: these had moved from one pile to another. Mariela acknowledged my new submissions with a sigh.

I went around to the other side of the office and approached Ron Turbide's cubicle. Ron had an insular manner. He didn't look up from his computer monitor but did acknowledge me with a shake of his head.

"Okay, this is every vendor statement from the past thirty days."

He reached sideways, accepted the papers, then set them onto the desk next to his keyboard.

I continued, "I guess, if you find anything not already in the system, let me know and I'll contact the vendor."

"No need. I'll phone and have them email copies. I'll send those so you can figure out what they are."

This was great—he was offering to take on more steps in the task. I said, "I really appreciate that."

"Myra should have been giving me these statements all along."

"Well, I'm glad to have your help now."

I left the business office, returned to the elevator, and rode down.

The nurse comes by to see how well Sam is gasping.

"How long will we be here?"

"The doctor will be through to talk with you. We need to observe his progress. He has to get something to eat."

"How can he, if he's down here?"

"You could try a bottle."

"Can't we take him back to his mother?"

"Ask the doctor."

I stay close, hovering over the baby's aquarium—the same size as fish-tanks I'd kept as a kid. Other babies have more elaborate fixtures: oxygen tanks, tubes of fluid. My baby is healthy by comparison. Wriggling and gasping—but less frantic. Settling into a rhythm. The electrodes are not in danger of popping off as he breathes somewhat steadily.

The doctor makes his way down my aisle. "You can give him a bottle if you want. He's hungry."

"But then won't he lose the ability to latch onto the breast?"

"Not necessarily. In any case, the way he's gasping he can't suckle now. He really should get something. You can delay for another hour, but probably nothing will change, and you'll give him the bottle anyway."

The naked baby covered with wires in the beeping room. We'd planned a birthing center; we'd imagined dim lights and soothing sounds.

"Then he could leave neonatal?"

"Yes, we could bring him back to his mother."

"Okay, give me a bottle."

The nurse returns with a half-sized plastic bottle of white milk. The huge translucent nipple seems impossibly dominant. A second nurse lifts my vulnerable child, trailing colored wires, and hands him to me. I accept the complicated body, cradling the loose head in my hand while supporting the torso on my forearm. With the other hand I grip the bottle and nuzzle the nipple at the baby's mouth.

Rapidly he engulfs and draws in milk. The sucking is furious: the whole body engaged in drinking.

"He was hungry," says the doctor. "But he's getting too much. Take it out."

I work the bottle out.

"You can give him some more now."

This time he pulls less quickly. But in a few more seconds the bottle is empty.

"Now you can go up to his mother."

Relaxed, though still gasping slightly, Sam is so intensely himself, his breathing a definitional rhythm, pulling in air and expelling it in elemental bursts.

Chris is in a semi-private suite. Sam lies beside her nipple breathing, not interested in the breast. The nurse offers Chris a small bottle.

"I gave him one. I know you're not supposed to, but they were going to monitor him in the neonatal ward pretty much until I did. It was so loud in there."

She doesn't protest but takes the bottle and offers it. Sam drinks rapidly again, and we share relief and confusion. We have failed to breastfeed at birth, and now it will be hard to get him started.

I'd arrived in the basement, resisted the call of the cafeteria on the left, turned right, and walked down the hallway to Facilities Manager Arnold Balmoral's office.

I poked my head in. He was seated, staring at his computer. "Hey Arnie, how's it going—you know this thing with the toilet in the bookstore—"

He looked up and smiled. "Yes Andy, Juan will be over today to look at it again. We'll get that taken care of for you."

"Thanks. You know, someone from OSHA called a few minutes ago saying they'd gotten an anonymous complaint from my staff about it."

He laughed and said, "Now that is what I would call turning the mundane into the monumental. Do not worry my friend, we'll fix it."

I reversed course, back down the hall, took the stairs up, whipped through the lobby, the turnstile, the successive front doors, onto 112th Street and west toward the bookstore but was brought up short by Phil Marciano on the sidewalk outside the door to our building's elevator lobby, disassembling two skids piled with boxes.

Phil looked up and said, "Toysmith, for Bulk Orders." I helped him transfer boxes off the skids into the lobby. Some of the Bulk Orders staff came down the elevator to participate, and I rode it up to the second floor. The back door had been propped open, and I entered, moved through to the sales floor, past the special orders desk to the large back room.

I noticed several more statements in the mail basket. Phil must have just opened more mail. I was agitated since these would be needed by Ron Turbide if he were to complete a full review today. I looked them over: there was nothing problematic, but I decided I needed to return to the business office immediately and hand them over. I darted back out toward the special orders desk but was stopped by my new best friend.

My friend blocked me—like the troll in *Three Billy Goats Gruff*—from the ramp that formed a narrow passage between the special orders desk and a spur of bookcases.

Waving a document, my best friend began to lecture, informing me that for twenty-five years, my predecessor had nurtured a valuable relationship with Scholastic Corporation, and in just a few short months I had irreparably destroyed that relationship.

My friend was only warming up. Continuing to shake the document, my friend alerted me that my failure to pay the bills I had heedlessly incurred had damaged the credit rating of Park Place College of Education. The Bulk Orders division was made to suffer and would be hindered by my failure to maintain what every bookseller knew was the minimal level of professional behavior.

I interrupted, "Let me see that."

My friend reminded me that I had been directly instructed by my supervisor to immediately repair the damage I had done to all of Park Place's vendor relationships—yet I failed to do this.

"That looks like one of those Scholastic ledgers. I'm heading back to the business office. I'll bring it." I lunged, grabbed the paper, sidled past, ran down the steps, and out the front door.

I ran around onto 112th Street, past the guys just finishing with the Toysmith boxes, through the sets of entry doors to the college, pulled out my wallet, scanned my ID card, through the turnstile, waved to Roger at the security desk, turned left toward the elevator, and punched the button. I waited.

The elevator arrived, I entered, punched seven, and rode up.

"*Samuel Laties is in custody of the Holyoke police.*"

I'd answered the door to find an Amherst police officer on the porch.

"Is he all right? What happened?"

"He's fine. He caused a disturbance on a bus: the driver radioed for assistance. You can pick him up at Holyoke Police Department on Appleton Street."

Twenty minutes later I'm at their counter. "Your son was rushing around inside the bus to West Springfield. Did not respond to driver's instructions. Driver thought he might be dangerous—pulled the bus over. Your son was compliant with us."

Down the hallway, nineteen-year-old Sam is seated, eyes shut. I hug him around the shoulders. "Did you get on the wrong bus from HCC?" *He nods.*

As we walk to the car he says, "When I saw it was going the other way, I tried to get off."

I reach for his hand. "I know. He should have figured and let you out. It's ridiculous he called the police."

The doors opened, I walked down the hall, turned left into the business office, and handed the additional documents to Ron. "Some more just came in. Sorry I didn't have these before. Could you particularly figure this one out?"

Ron accepted the papers wordlessly, barely moving.

"Thanks," I said. I walked back out, nodding to Mariela on my way. I went down the hall, punched the elevator button, waited, entered, and punched one.

"Sam must remain here," says Offia Nwali. For the past week, he's been witness to Sam's tics, OCD, and flashes of conversational brilliance. "Sam will have a cow. They will roam the countryside together. Wherever Sam goes, the village will look after him."

Turning down such an offer from Offia Nwali cannot be a casual thing. He's a former senator and the traditional leader of the Ezza people, with a doctorate from Harvard. He's also family: my brother-in-law's brother-in-law. Thirteen-year-old Sam and I have been visiting for the past week.

Sam had asked to visit this village in the rainforest of Eastern Nigeria after hearing of it from my sister Claire's sister-in-law, Susan Davis. She and Offia had fallen in love in 1959, at Brown University. They'd married thirty-six years later, a decade after the tragic death in a plane crash of Offia's first wife and kids, which had triggered his departure from national government: he'd returned to his ancestral village of Ameka, taking up his role as traditional leader.

I'd been planning for us to go back to Costa Rica for Sam's thirteenth-birthday trip—but I was delighted when Sam responded so warmly to Susan's glowing description of life in Ameka. We had all traveled here together.

It's true Sam has been rising early to roam. Yesterday I caught a glimpse of him through the trees: Sam's chin was pointed skyward in his usual, unusual way, and a dozen small children were trailing behind, mimicking. I knew they weren't teasing, the way some kids at school did. These children were having fun hanging around Sam.

I imagine Sam herding his cow day after lazy Ameka day, receiving spiritual and intellectual guidance from the remarkable Offia Nwali. In America, the older Sam gets, the more his life could be a competitive, win-or-lose, succeed-or-fail affair. I am worried for him. "Let me check," I reply to Offia.

I mention to Sam that he's been invited to live in the village. There's a cow in it for him.

"Dad," is all Sam says.

A week later we're back in our Near North Side townhouse, and he's on the computer playing Age of Empires.

* * *

SON OF REBEL BOOKSELLER

I walked through the lobby, the turnstile, the two sets of front doors, onto 112th Street.

The Toysmith boxes were gone. I guessed that Phil had brought the wooden skids themselves into the college's garbage bay. I went around to the store's front entrance on Broadway, greeted Asha at the cash register, headed upstairs to the large back room, and steeled myself for another encounter with my new best friend.

My friend must have retreated to the Bulk Orders lair.

Our warehouse hallway was jammed with the dozens of Toysmith boxes for Conquest Academies plus a large shipment from Playmobil just delivered by UPS for the retail store.

My assistant manager Heidi French was in the buying office with a commissioned sales rep, ordering more toys. She'd arrived for a twelve-noon shift that would take her through closing at ten. I'd be leaving at six: I had dinner plans.

Juan Rodriguez approached, carrying a large coiled plumbing snake, to let me know he'd be working on the toilet. After a minute, as I chatted with Heidi and her rep, Juan was waving through the office door. "I'm coming back with Warren, Señor."

I went into the large back room, sat at my desk, and tried to organize the piles of catalogs and paperwork Phil had tossed there.

Fifteen-year-old Sam writes for the North Star newsletter:

I moved from Chicago to Amherst last August. In eighth grade in Chicago I became very shy around people. I was so shy that I was unable to fit into a group. People teased me. My parents took me out of school.

We began to think about where I would go to high school in Amherst. There was always the regular public school. Then I discovered another option online. North Star is a place where students design their own curricula for the personal path of learning they want to pursue.

Many people sit around on the sofas and talk about all sorts of interesting things. Sometimes kids play banjoes. At North Star everyone knows everyone else. Everyone is friendly.

I wrote a paper on late 19th century German Industrialism. I learned about the Paris Commune of 1870. We just read One Flew Over the Cuckoo's Nest. *I compose poetry. We discuss current politics.*

I am happy because of the relaxed social and academic environment. There is no social pressure. Cliques do not exist.

I heard Warren's Jamaican accent from the sales floor. A moment later, I heard laughter coming from the direction of the bathroom. Warren looked into the back room. A smile on his face, he said, "Mister Andy, come look."

I followed him into the bathroom, where Juan was standing next to the toilet tank. The tank lid was on the floor leaning against the wall. Juan held up a wad of toilet paper.

"Señor," Juan began, "this was inside here." I approached, and Juan showed me how the cylinder inside the tank through which water must flow had been blocked by the wad of paper. Juan said, "Someone put it there."

I looked him in the face. I turned and looked Warren in the face. We all started laughing.

Juan said, "Someone was playing a joke on you, Señor."

Warren said, "Andy, candy, jack-a-dandy, someone has been having a laugh."

"Thank you both. At least we don't have to pay the plumber."

Juan and Warren left. I took down the "Out of Order" sign from the bathroom door.

I sidled up to Phil at his receiving desk and said, "You heard that?"

"Warren told me."

Robert Mandala had arrived; Phil got him started receiving the Playmobil order. I decided to give Asha a break at the cash register.

As I rang a customer, my new best friend descended the staircase and approached, asking who was telephoning our vendors right now. I had been specifically instructed to do this and I was violating my supervisor's direct order.

"Ron in the business office is doing it."

My friend seemed slightly shaken, but recovered, mumbling, "Well, isn't that an efficient way to run a bookstore," before retreating up the stairs.

The phone rang. "Park Place Bookstore, this is Andy."

"Hi honey, how's your day?" Rebecca asked.

"Well, I had a feeling this was going to be a strange one—I've been taking notes—but—I can't talk in public."

"Sounds interesting. Are you all right?"

"Yeah, but you need to ask tonight."

"That's why I called. Since you're going to be having dinner with Sarah and Chris, I decided to see if Sylvan and Jess wanted to get together with me. We're meeting near Cooper at nine."

I was ringing a customer. "That's wonderful, I'm glad you're—I've got to—"

"Wait, that's only part of why I called. I wanted to let you know I'm heading to Chelsea now with that deposit."

Rebecca had decided to move the R.L. Migdal Multimedia team out of our apartment's dining room and into a loft on the sixth floor of an arts building. It was a share: four-hundred square feet of a space that housed manufacturing and design tenants. I said, "That's great—and give Sylvan and Jessica my love."

The phone rings: "Chicago Children's Museum Store, this is Andy."
    "Dad?"
    "Sam! What's up?"
    "I'm at the top of the Sears Tower."
    He is eleven. I've taught him to use public transit; he roams all over town.
    "Can you see me down here at Navy Pier?"
    "Dad? I'm gonna walk there."
    "From Sears, really? That's a long walk."
    "Okay, bye."
    I know it's a scorcher. Two hours later he shows up, his face red. Behind the counter with me, he flops on the floor-mat.
    "Sam, I can't believe it—you came two miles from the top of Sears Tower? Did you fly?"
    He's sweaty and panting. "I had to sit down on the sidewalk after every block."

Asha returned; I went upstairs to my desk in the large back room.
    I watched Phil stickering books at the receiving table.

Click, click, click. Four-year-old Sam puts a sticker on another book with our manual pricing gun. His $0.01 price stickers

are always turning up on books when people bring them to the register.
  Click, click, click. "Daddy," he asks, "why are guns bad?"

"Today is Sam's birthday."
  Phil turned. "Oh, yeah? How old?"
  "Twenty-six."
  "What was it again?"
  "Drug interaction—seizure—then they fucked up in the ambulance."
  He was looking at me.
  "We counted the pills, after."
  He turned to his work. "You doing anything?"
  "I'm having dinner with my daughter and ex-wife—she's coming down from Amherst."
  Over his shoulder, he remarked, "You still talking with your ex-wife? That's nice for your daughter."
  "We're going to tell each other stories about him; he would have liked that."
  Phil was the only one I'd talked with about Sam's unusual psychological profile, because when we'd met, Phil had told me his own diagnosis.
  "Phil," I hazarded, "I want to let you know that from now on, I'm going to give statements and publisher notices to Ron in the business office." To my relief, Phil said, "Sounds good."

At three in the morning, twenty-year-old Sam wakes up. "Dad? I need to go back."
  A curtained room in the Cooley-Dick intensive care unit. I've been half-asleep in a chair, but I'm wide awake now.
  "Sam—you're talking. You must have the perfect level of Clozaril in your bloodstream. You want to do some planning?"

He's looking straight ahead with a thoughtful gaze. "I'm going back to the Berkshire Center. I know I can do it." He has spent the past few months—on and off—in Lee, Massachusetts, at a residential center for college-aged young people with learning differences.

"It would be your third time over there. You need help with your meds. This thing of skipping doses and catching up with a week's worth could kill you. Can we hire a nurse to come each day? You said no before, but—"

"Okay, I don't care. I just need to go back."

We talk for an hour—the most in some time. He explains his plan: he'll earn credits at Berkshire Community College, then transfer into University of Massachusetts.

He subsides into silence. The Clozaril is wearing off.

I decided to get lunch. I went downstairs and out onto Broadway, then two doors down to Samad's. At the sandwich counter, I ordered hummus on pita with lettuce and tomato. The guy was surprised, because I usually got tuna. I shrugged and did not explain that Sam was vegetarian.

Sam, aged six, is telling a startled hot-dog vendor why not to eat meat: it's mean to animals, rainforests get cut, cow-farts pollute, people get heart attacks, and cows eat food hungry kids need.

I waited for my order, reflexively checking the phone. There was indeed a new email, addressed to Vince and copying me, complaining that the bookstore had received threatening notices from Simon & Schuster and Scholastic.

Standing in line at Samad's, I typed a response on my phone, informing Vince that neither of these documents were late notices, but rather artifacts of the vendors' receivables systems. There were no problems here.

I returned to the bookstore, went up to the large back room and sat down in the breaktime area. Asha Phillips was reading a book while having lunch. As we ate, I said, "You are the person whose drawers always balance to the penny."

"Really?"

"You stay focused when everything is crazy."

I checked my phone for more email unpleasantness and saw that Vice President Ben Daniel had written. He suggested I help him create a proposal to rework the bookstore into a neighborhood literacy center for the science campus that Columbia University was building in West Harlem. I already knew that—unfortunately—there'd be a gap of years between the end of our current lease and the availability of a finished storefront on the new science campus. I typed a response into my phone, asking to get together.

Three weeks before, I'd written a formal memo to the college executives and trustees, making the case for store relocation—as trustee Albert Rollins last May had warned I'd need to do. Since I was failing to cut the deficit with higher sales or lower staff costs, the main hope we had left was paying less rent. I requested that we start the search for a new storefront. Amid the daily distraction, I'd striven to focus.

Eleven-year-old Sam reports for The Jeff's Class Tribune:

WHAT PEOPLE LIKE ABOUT THE CLASS AND WHAT THEY WOULD LIKE CHANGED

What Sydney wants is that people would not get so goofy at the end of the day and she wants Jeff to be in a better mood at

the end of the day. Ray thinks we should ban Pokemon forever. Jenni likes that people are nice, and the teachers are cool, and that we don't get a lot of math books. She wants cleanup to run smoother and she wants to get a mammal for a pet. Drew says he would like kids not to be so rude. The following two people wish to be anonymous: One said he/she wants more recess, and Gameboys back. Two wants to get dismissed at 8:45 AM. Two actually likes something. To tell you the truth, he/she likes more than one thing. Those things are lunch, recess, and after-school.

I'd returned to the downstairs sales floor. Dara Andante introduced me to a former employee who now worked training teachers at forty high schools. I knew she was far from the only accomplished former staffer in the history of our store—founded in the '50s, in the West Village—and I suggested we create an alumni page on our website. Dara recalled that our former bookseller Jen Brennan had coined a phrase to describe the powerhouse children's lit experts of the bookstore: GLOPPs, which stood for "Great Ladies of Park Place." Jen Brennan herself had left in 2006 to help create and run the Thalia's Book Club children's author series at Symphony Space, for which Park Place Bookstore had continued to serve as co-producer.

My three o'clock appointment had arrived. Allen Sapphire was a documentary maker hoping Park Place Bookstore would host showings of his *Inquiring Youngster* films about early childhood progressive education. He'd produced these at the Child Development Institute of Sarah Lawrence College. We went upstairs and settled into some chairs left out since storyhour.

Allen showed me part of one of the movies, on his laptop. Since I was an SLC dad myself—Sarah was class of 2011—I knew Sarah Lawrence College shared with Park Place a role as leading force in the field of progressive education. I agreed we'd be a great place to screen Allen's videos.

We talked for a while. I found myself describing my frustration selling so many expensive test-prep products to anxious young parents. I felt high stakes testing of preschoolers was a form of child abuse. Yet on arriving at Park Place Bookstore I'd learned I would be running a robust sales program in the category. Getting into a good preschool in Manhattan was a matter of getting a good score, and many parents wished to discipline their three-year-olds to succeed on the bizarre tests. We were one of the few stores that stocked a line of forty-dollar, forty-page paperback books that closely tracked the content of these secret tests. In fact, these test-prep paperbacks were the famously progressive Park Place Bookstore's bestselling books! It seemed the height of hypocrisy. Yes, as a bookseller, I felt if parents demanded these items, I would sell them. I tried not to be intolerant of their choices, but I wasn't good at concealing my feelings.

It's eleven at night, and our crowded plane from Miami is circling O'Hare in a snowstorm. I've allowed three-year-old Sam to tramp up and down the aisles while I tag along, eliciting irritated glares from fellow passengers. No one is despised like a parent who fails to control his child.

As the plane circles, I now hold Sam on my lap and read aloud Arnold Lobel's Grasshopper on the Road. *Among the characters Grasshopper meets are a parade of beetles marching in support of morning. They welcome Grasshopper when he says he likes morning but are furious when he adds that afternoon and night are also nice. Reading Lobel makes me feel better about being disliked for my parenting style. There are many ways to be a parent; being supportive and indulgent is my way.*

Allen continued to draw me out, and I realized I was talking about Sam. I explained we'd enrolled him at Waldorf and Montessori schools to ensure the arts were central to his education—and to shield him from standardized testing and test prep. Sam had especially benefitted from Near North Montessori's support of the newspaper he'd launched.

"My Schooling," getting better.

Three grade levels were brought together in one room (fourth, fifth and sixth). Students selected a good deal of their own work, organized their own projects and moved at will around the rather large classroom. In addition to this were group lessons that were followed by homework. This whole arrangement suited me much better than before, giving me above all mobility. I conceived The Jeff's Class Tribune, *a newspaper covering class events and school news. That newspaper was the most important work I did, mainly because it let me make friends. Throughout this period my general focus was on work; it was very enjoyable for me.*

Sam's drive to write had grown so strong that after school let out in May of '99, he'd spent six weeks crafting what turned out to be his magnum opus: a funny, Kafkaesque tale of a boy who buys homework from a corrupt website. He'd finished just in time to send it, as promised, to the school learning specialist, before we left town for a late-June trip to New York.

SON OF REBEL BOOKSELLER

* * *

"Don't go near the edge!"
    We've ridden the escalator from the observation deck out onto the roof. Twelve-year-old Sam, exhilarated, has darted against the wind across the top of the Twin Tower toward the brink. It's a hundred stories down.
    Safe back indoors, we circle the windows, taking in the city of toys from a quarter mile up, then head for the elevator.
    As we wait in line, a photographer is snapping portraits of everyone. I don't want to be forced to buy a touristy photo, but Sam strikes a joyful pose and the camera clicks.
    At ground level, we emerge. The photo is displayed: Sam flying. I buy it.

Unfortunately, it had proven impossible to shield teenaged Sam from standardized tests, and his chronic anxiety had resulted—for instance—in a zero on his SAT essay, and a hundred-and-two on his IQ test. Crazy, considering what a good writer he was—and so smart! Those scores had damaged his self-esteem.

"We won, and I got the highest score," seventeen-year-old Sam reports. It's amazing enough that he joined the Amherst High School debate team, attended practice, and participated in a tournament. Now this!
    "Sam! How wonderful for you!"
    The next evening, when I peek into his room after dinner: "Dad, you know what I told you yesterday about the debate team? We didn't really win."
    "Oh?"
    "We almost did, but—we lost, because of me."

"Oh, Sam."

"We were ahead, and it was my turn, and I didn't say anything. So, the whole team lost."

I told Allen about Park Place Bookstore's paradoxical situation at that moment. The retail storefront was losing money, but our Bulk Orders division was selling to Conquest Academies, which operated in a manner I found antithetical to Park Place's ideas. Bulk Orders was creating centrally programmed classroom libraries, but I felt effective classroom collections were composed of titles selected by individual teachers. To boot, one element of the Conquest business was toys for some sort of student bribery program I didn't understand. I only knew from our point of sale system that tens of thousands of dollars in toys had already this year been sold to Conquest, and the program was called "incentives."

Allen and I discussed his films. I suggested we show them during the weeks of the Reading and Writing Institutes held by Columbia University's Teachers College every summer. These programs, operated by Professor Lucy Calkins, drew thousands of children's-literature-loving educators from around the country. Hundreds of these teachers visited Park Place Bookstore during lunch breaks to shop with our expert booksellers, or later in the day to enjoy our wine-and-cheese mixers. We penciled in dates for Allen's screenings.

I walked Allen downstairs and noticed, with alarm, an interdepartmental envelope that had been left at the register. It contained a bill from the office supply company Staples.

I'd never been told exactly how to pay this vendor. Some operations bills were supposed to be submitted with a cover sheet, as if they were regular vendor payables, but some were supposed to be put onto the bookstore's credit card. In this vexed moment, I decided not to take a chance.

I headed out the door after Allen, said goodbye to him, ran to the college, in through the two sets of doors, pulled out my wallet, scanned my ID, through the turnstile, turned left through the lobby to the elevator, punched the button, waited, got in, and punched seven.

"My Schooling," getting worse.

In late February of sixth grade my OCD struck for a second time, but now rather than religious vows it was (and is) characterized by thoughts of a horrific nature that randomly and uncontrollably occur in my head. These thoughts got (and get) louder and louder in my head until I am unable to distinguish between them and normal speech. This left me marooned on a rock with waves of work tumbling over me. I became unable to cope with all of it.

I'd walked down the hall and turned left into the business office. I asked Mariela, "Hi—I see you sent this to me—could you please tell me if I'm supposed to pay it with the credit card?"

Ron Turbide stood up, in his cubicle around the other side from Mariela's. "You just put the cover sheet on and fill it out!" Mariela was looking at him with alarm. "Before I came to Park Place, I worked for a two-hundred-million-dollar a year company. Do you realize how small your bookstore is? Why do you think you are so important? You give us more and more invoices, and does Vince hire us any extra help? Then the more you give us to do, the more upset you get." He glanced at Mariela and seemed to calm down a little. "Look, I know it's not you—"

Mariela clarified, in her soft Filipino accent, "You-Know-Who comes—stands here—to tell us..."

I was surprised. "I get that too!"

Ron said, "You're not making enough money to justify all this work. The college should close the bookstore instead of piling this on. Your charter school business isn't worth it."

"You think the Conquest thing isn't making a profit?"

"Your budgets aren't being charged for us. If you had to pay—"

He broke off and sat down.

"Can I do the Staples paperwork right now?"

Mariela handed me the cover sheet, I filled it out and passed back the submission. "Thank you both. I'm sorry it's such a nuisance. I support the idea that the college should hire an extra person to help with the bookstore's data input, since Bulk Orders is growing so much."

I went out to the hallway, over to the elevator, punched the button, and waited.

Chris and I have been called to a meeting with Sam's teacher, who is a longtime friend.

We peek into the class. At the front corner of the thirty-desk room, in his seat, ten-year-old Sam is twitching.

Frances wraps up and comes to the door. In the meeting, she tells us Sam has changed. She tries to calm us: he has merely become eccentric.

That night, I sit on Sam's bed. "What's it like?"

"I have to bet my soul to the devil. If I cough once and jump once, the devil can't take my soul straight to hell." He demonstrates a quick cough and twitch.

"The devil?"

"I don't want to make the bet, so I say, 'I won't bet my soul to the devil,' over and over."

"You have to keep saying 'I won't bet my soul to the devil' to keep the bets from happening?"

"If I don't say it fast enough, I make the bet."

"And the bet—when it happens—is when the devil—?"

"The bet says, if I don't cough once and jump once, then the devil can take my soul straight to hell."

He coughs and twitches.

The elevator doors opened in the basement. I got out, turned right, toward Facilities Manager Arnie Balmoral's office, and peeked in, but he wasn't there this time. I turned around, went up the steps to street level, out toward the front desk, and saw Arnie standing there talking with Roger.

Arnie smiled and said, "Well, Andy—Juan told me about your toilet. I wonder who would do something like that?"

"I don't know, but I think it ought to be in one of our books."

"All's well that ends well," Arnie concluded.

I headed back through the turnstile, through the two sets of doors, east on 112th Street, back to the store's front door, in, said hello to Asha at the cash register, and up the steps. I went behind the upstairs register, which we weren't operating that day, and pulled up my email account.

Yes, my best friend was informing Vince that I refused to follow Vince's directive that I be the one to personally call vendors.

As many times before, I puzzled about this person. I speculated that my best friend wanted me fired for insubordination, so I did not get credit for a bookstore that survived only thanks to Bulk Orders profits.

I emailed Vince, copying my friend, that from now on I would respond only once each day to these emails, and from now on I'd bring all paperwork to Ron Turbide for evaluation.

I looked up to see a tall man approaching. He had a facial tic that reminded me of Sam. He introduced himself, told me he was completing his Masters in Library Science, and asked if there were any jobs. I suggested he apply in the fall, when I could hire full-time help. He was happy to hear this and assured me he'd be back.

I thought about the challenges this man was overcoming, collecting an advanced degree while managing Tourette's syndrome. I hadn't told him my son had also suffered from OCD and Tourette's.

Nineteen-year-old Sam keeps a journal of his college days.

Mon, September 17: Day in Review.
Today I went to GCC [Greenfield Community College] for my psychology class. Because I was three hours early, I sat on a park bench and read the psychology textbook. Later I read the US foreign relations textbook. I don't think I should have been reading the US foreign relations textbook at GCC because of the political nature of its content. At any rate I am caught up for Tuesday's foreign policy homework.

When I put the foreign policy book down and went to class, I found I was twenty minutes late. In the future I must be more mindful of the time. I was forced therefore, by my own negligence, to take the GCC bus to the Greenfield town center. From there, I went on to Northampton, and from there to the movie theater. Mom picked me up at the movie theater.

Today was stressful because I had taken less medication than usual. The purpose of lowering the med dose for a day was to gauge my response to less medication. I won't try it again.

*   *   *

The need to censor myself about Sam was constant. Usually, I thought to mention Sam when working with someone who had a teen that sounded like him. I'd suggest long walks together to get them talking (Sam: Chicago lakefront); music lessons (Sam: trombone); reading historical fiction out loud (Sam: *I, Claudius*). But the times I'd brought up Sam with customers had gone badly—I'd always wished I could back up. A bereaved father brings conversations to a terrible standstill.

I'd probably never learn not to talk about Sam—but I'd succeeded this time.

I was still at the second-floor register. Jennifer Brown was coming upstairs. "Andy, I was hoping to catch you. We just got confirmation: we're getting Neil Gaiman, Jon Klassen, and Lemony Snicket for a joint launch of *The Dark*."

"Jennifer! That's impossible."

She was beaming, "It will be in the auditorium. School for Children families only—it's not open to the public, but we'll livestream it. We're hoping the bookstore can do pre-sales to parents. We'll have the authors sign before the show."

"So, you don't need us to run a table in the lobby?"

"No, we're going to tell parents they have to pre-order. If that works for you?"

Jennifer Brown coordinated Park Place Children's Literature Committee, Park Place Writers Group and Park Place Center for Children's Books—each a separate entity with a unique story. The bookstore frequently handled book sales for her in the college lobby, during awards ceremonies and festivals.

Park Place College's role as generative hub and critical voice in the field of children's literature stemmed from its founder's irritation with the quality of children books in the 1920s. Graduate student Margaret Wise Brown—who later wrote *Goodnight Moon*—had been tasked with spearheading the initiative to create books grounded in children's immediate experience.

How many times as a child, and decades later as a parent, had I read those hundreds of Park Place-inspired books, like *The Carrot Seed*, *Harold and the Purple Crayon*, most of the *Little Golden Books*, and *Where the Wild Things Are?*

The Harper and Row hotel suite at the American Booksellers Association convention, Washington DC, 1987. Jennifer Brown and my sister Nancy are colleagues. Sitting somberly in an armchair facing away from the group is Maurice Sendak, author of Where the Wild Things Are. *I am introduced. He says, "Hello," then looks with interest into two-month-old Sam's alert eyes, and—after several seconds—remarks, "A real child."*

Two hours before, Sam had attended the Children's Book and Author Breakfast with two thousand booksellers and publishers. He was in Nancy's arms, with my mom and dad, at our family's table. Chris and I were up on the dais accepting the Women's National Book Association's Pannell Award. We'd been named the booksellers who'd done the most to bring children and books together in 1986.

Myra Raines had recently recalled that morning to me. "That rat ran across the stage while you guys were up there."

"A rat?"

"No-one told you? We all thought it was great."

Now—nearly twenty-six years since that day—Jennifer runs Park Place's children's lit programs, Nancy is chair of the Children's Book Council, Chris and I are divorced—she's at Eric Carle Museum and I'm here, trying to save Myra's bookstore.

Maurice died last year—and Sam—

*   *   *

Jennifer was gone. Heidi French approached. "Andy—did you see those middle-schoolers with backpacks who were hovering around the Hexbugs while you were talking with Jennifer?"

"No, what?"

"They were stealing. I restocked this display today. Look at it now!"

"I'm sorry. I was distracted I guess."

"Today you haven't been paying attention to customers. You're sitting around talking. Well, what are we going to do? We need more security cameras. You know, those kids have been here before."

I told Heidi I'd request that Juan put a camera at the top of the steps, and then asked her, "Is it always the people you're trying to help who become your parasites?"

She stared at me, replied, "I don't know, but I think we should watch out for those kids," and walked toward the back.

I checked my email again. Ron Turbide had written.

There were no problems with the vendor statements. However—in the case of the Scholastic document which my best friend had been upset about, Ron had news. One invoice from a few months ago was problematic. Ron had obtained a copy; it was attached.

I opened the attachment. This was for a Bulk Orders purchase. My best friend was the one who'd failed to submit.

I wrote Ron, thanking him. I forwarded Ron's email to Vince, copying my best friend, explaining that Ron Turbide's analysis revealed no significant issues—and the sole problem didn't involve me.

I felt bathed in vindication.

Ugh.

It was six. I got my coat from the large back room, wished Heidi luck, and headed downtown for Sam's birthday dinner.

14—A VERY LARGE HOMEWORK ASSIGNMENT: CHAPTER FIVE—ONE ELATED WEB SITE OWNER

The man with the bald spot got up from his desk and went over to the owner's office, and after he had jealously admired the fancy trappings of the office, the plush carpet, the vaulted ceilings, the many portraits of the owner—the man who sat behind the silver-plated desk with the gold pen-holder—he went up to the desk.

"What do you have for me today, Alfrate (the bald man's name)?" The owner was very fat, and always dressed in a large tuxedo.

Alfrate was talking fast, "I— I—" he stuttered, "I've just completed a five-thousand-dollar transaction. A hundred-page report!"

The owner's—whose real name was Avarerus Leuarious, but everyone just called him Boss—eyes lit up. "Did you say five thousand dollars? And since I own twenty percent of the company, that means I get one thousand dollars! And that's just enough to finish my down payments for that vacation to Paris in the Concorde, yes, yes, this is definitely good."

"The problem is," Alfrate said, "it has to be done by six-thirty tomorrow morning."

"All right, then it'll be done by six-thirty tomorrow morning," Avarerus said, leaning forward. "And you're going to make sure it gets done by six-thirty tomorrow morning...or, well, there are other people that would like your job."

"Yes, Boss."

"Since this is such a big project, and it needs to be done so soon, you can have fifteen writers."

"Thank you," Alfrate said hastily. "I'll need them."

"You can have the fifteen in Sector H. And you can write the outline yourself. Get up, get out of here, there's not a minute to be wasted!"

"Yes, Boss," Alfrate said, as he got up from the silk-covered chair and walked out of the velvet-colored door.

How was he going to do this? If this thing wasn't finished in ten hours, then his goose would be cooked. How would he feed his family?

Well, there was no time to be wasted thinking about his family. He had to sit down and write an outline. So, he did sit down and wrote an outline.

About twenty minutes later it was finished. It started something like this:

    I   Introduction
    II   Civilizations 3-8000 B.C.
    A   Eurasia
    I.   Europe Area
    i.   Spain Area
    a.   Tribes in Spain area

It went on and on. In total, it was about fifteen pages long.

Alfrate got up and went over to the elevator. The people who would write this report, i.e. Sector H, were on the fourteenth floor of this fifteen-floor building.

When the elevator door opened, Alfrate walked into it and pressed fourteen.

It was an old elevator, and creaked as it went up.

Alfrate had always thought they should enter the elevator in a contest for The Guinness Book of World Records. *It would probably win the title of Slowest Elevator of All Time.*

But Alfrate's mind wasn't on the elevator. It was on his job. And if he could keep it. Frankly, he just wasn't quite sure if he or Sector H could get this job done. It was such a large project, and it had to be done so soon. Even if fifteen people were working on it simultaneously, could it really be finished in the elected time-period? He just wasn't sure.

The elevator had reached the fourth floor. He'd left from the second.

Maybe he should just take the stairs. That would be the best idea.

He got out at four and walked up to fourteen.

There it was just as busy as it was on the second floor. The floor was divided into four sectors. J, P, H and E. It was so confusing: the sectors were in no particular order so a certain sector could be on almost any floor.

Alfrate walked over to where Sector H was. Before he got there, he realized something, but he wasn't really sure what.

What was it?

There was something about Sector H.

What was it?

He was still walking toward it. He was almost there. But there was something he couldn't remember about Sec—

Oh no, not Sector H!

Now he was sure he would lose his job.

Oh God, Why? Why? This couldn't be happening to him. Anything but Sector H!

Sector H was where all the German immigrants who had probably never learned English tenses, were. They would also sometimes mess up their words. Oh God, this was going to be really painful.

Alfrate sighed, because he knew the boss would not give him another group of writers, because he never did that.

He'd reached Sector H. So Alfrate went over to the buzzer, that, when pressed, was supposed to get everyone's attention, but rarely did.

He pressed it anyway.

15—MALPRACTICE

I had an unfortunate record of collecting traffic tickets while unloading boxes for New York City offsite events, but I had to risk it: I'd already spent twenty minutes in stop-and-go traffic circling the huge McGraw-Hill Center, on the corner of 48th Street and Avenue of the Americas. Clicking on my blinkers, I leapt out and loaded my little red two-wheeler with three boxes of books and a crate of check-out supplies. I rolled the hand-truck up a ramp, humped it over a few steps, then in through plate-glass doors to the elegant lobby. I left everything next to the sales tables, ran back to my van, and drove to a garage. No ticket for me.

By the time I was back, more Park Placers were arriving: Ben Daniel was managing event logistics and President Wright would be introducing the featured guest. This annual Park Place lecture honored the college's first president. Today's speaker was Diane Ravitch, who'd been Assistant Secretary of Education under President George H. W. Bush.

Diane Ravitch was now a professor of education at New York University. In the '90s and 2000s, she'd been one of the school reform movement's most prominent advocates, favoring more charter schools to promote school choice, the increased use of high-stakes standardized testing, and George W. Bush's "No Child Left Behind" program.

However, in 2010 Diane Ravitch had reversed course, declaring that the school reform movement had failed. She'd written *The Death and Life of the Great American School*

System, and begun a vigorous campaign advocating a return to the strategy of aspiring to provide better funding for all public schools, implementing smaller class sizes, and offering more training and freedom for teachers in the classroom.

Today's lecture topic was "What New York's Next Mayor Needs to Know." While Conquest Academies founder Linda Lasch had announced that she was not running this year, she'd told the press she was aiming for a mayoral run in 2017. So, I was hopeful Diane Ravitch would express her opinions about Conquest Academies.

I was not disappointed. During her speech and the subsequent panel discussion, Professor Ravitch said the next mayor should visit Park Place for inspiration, and that in contrast, Conquest Academies' approach represented "educational malpractice."

Afterwards, as I sat next to Diane Ravitch—handling book sales during her signing—I was sorely tempted to reveal the story of Park Place Bookstore's "incentives" business with Conquest Academies. But I didn't feel I could, given my lack of knowledge of the program's exact character.

At birth, Sam suffers from kinked eustachian tubes. This leads to ear infections: he needs antibiotics.

The pediatrician proposes to implant ear tubes, allowing fluid to drain. I don't want tiny Sam to suffer surgery. The doctor agrees the issue might resolve naturally.

Next winter, the ear infection recurs. We try several antibiotics in succession: first-generation, penicillin; second-generation, Ceclor; third-generation, Suprax. Problem finally solved. Again, the doctor mentions ear tubes; again, I feel we should allow nature to deal with this.

Sam is five, and has endured ear infections and antibiotics each winter, before I decide ear tubes are inevitable. After surgery, as I view him sedated, I feel glad we hadn't done it when he was just a baby.

Five years later, standing in Borders bookstore in Evanston, reading through the psychology section in search of answers about obsessive-compulsive disorder, I encounter a discussion of PANDAS: Pediatric Autoimmune Neuropsychiatric Disorders Associated with Streptococcal Infections. Excessive use of strong antibiotics in early childhood has been implicated in onset of obsessive-compulsive disorder and Tourette's.

I feel shock, grief, guilt and denial. Had my fear of subjecting Sam to surgery condemned him to lifelong torment?

In the past, I'd been guilty of waiting for a serious problem to resolve itself. But sometimes, things get much worse. Determining whether Park Place College was selling toys to Conquest Academies for use as unethical bribes could not be delayed. If I sleuthed around in folders on the bookstore's shared Google Drive, maybe I'd find something that documented the Conquest Academies toy buying.

It was easier than I'd expected. The memo I found was titled "2012-2013 Test Prep Incentives—Overview." It was a granular, sophisticated plan for calibrated distribution of toys as prizes during many weeks of test prep. Incentives would be given out on a weekly basis, increasing in cost as the state tests approached. They would arrive in labeled boxes from Park Place. Each teacher would have a 'prize box' in their classroom to use at the teacher's discretion.

The previous year, John Ayers had written in response to my query about Conquest Academies, "Many charters become test prep factories and can churn out good numbers, but the lasting educational value is questionable. I really don't know if they are like this." Now I had evidence that Linda Lasch was getting her well-known high test-scores by using huge quantities of toys as crude rewards to turn students into rote performers. Months that should have been devoted to stimulating curiosity, celebrating creativity, and motivating a love of learning were being squandered in a carnival of trivial pursuit. School was about giving the right answers and being rewarded with prizes.

Since Ben Daniel was one of the retail bookstore's supporters, and he'd also been the lead organizer for the lecture, I decided Ben was the person most likely to respond to my scandalous discovery. I forwarded him the memo.

> APRIL 10, 2013
> TO: BEN DANIEL. EMAIL SUBJECT: TESTING INCENTIVE PROGRAM AT CONQUEST ACADEMIES
> This is the program for which Park Place Bookstore has provided over $70,000 in merchandise already this year. 1,500 students at about $50 worth of toys per student. This business has increased a lot since last year and as this chain of schools continues to grow, this part of the business with Park Place will also continue to grow.

Ben wrote back, "Interesting. Thanks for sending this."

I felt that Ben didn't seem sufficiently interested. I tried to capture his attention further by sending him a link to a recent *Wall Street Journal* article with some of my own commentary:

> LINK: June 26, 2012—"Lasch Delays a Run: Charter-schools operator Linda Lasch wants to run for mayor. Just not in 2013."

What's strange about our situation is that IF she is elected mayor then presumably it would be good for Park Place to have been on her side while she was rolling out her charter schools. But, what if during her campaign she is attacked for "educational malpractice" (as Diane Ravitch did during that speech) and she points to Park Place as a defense of her pedagogy (as she does in her memoir). Does this mean Park Place has to cover for her use of toys as bribes during aggressive test prep? This practice is not mentioned in her book (published last year)—in fact there is no entry for "Test" in the book's index and nothing about it in the book that I could see. She spends most of the book emphasizing reading.

Ben responded that the idea of Mayor Linda was too scary to contemplate and, fortunately, it was unlikely.

I was getting nowhere with him. I wrote back, "Ok thanks. What I need from keeping you in this particular loop is simply to feel sure that I am not collaborating with Conquest Academy in their appalling pedagogy by failing to alert the college to what seems peculiar to me about it."

By summer, a clear message was coming from President Wright about the bookstore.

First, Vince Tower requested that I prepare a "web-only" bookstore business plan.

Then, interim Vice President for Finance William Wilson, who was stepping into the administration from his post as a board trustee, asked me directly during a meeting in Vince Tower's office, "How fast can we shut the bookstore down? Can we do it this year?"

A few weeks later, when I'd failed to present the beginnings of the web-only bookstore plan, Vince told me that President Wright had assigned this task to trustee Tess Benson. During August, Tess prepared a plan and I saw drafts of it. I couldn't read the entire thing. Our past year of website development and online marketing had aimed to supplement the storefront, not supplant it.

In October, the board voted to approve a retail bookstore strategy framed by trustee Albert Rollins. The existing lease would not be renewed. Any new storefront location must be in the same neighborhood and have a rent no higher than two-hundred-thousand dollars per year: almost sixty percent below the bookstore's current rent. If no such location could be contracted, the bookstore would close.

This board decision, without the financial specifics, was communicated by President Wright to the full Park Place community in an e-newsletter. Luckily, one recipient was *New York Times Book Review* editor Pamela Paul, whose son had been enrolled in a Park Place program. Paul tweeted the news. Her tweet triggered coverage in *Publishers Weekly*, *Columbia Spectator* and other media.

At Christmastime, the Bulk Orders division moved out of our back rooms to a warehouse in North Harlem. My best friend informed me that Bulk Orders was going to be taking all the bookstore's vendor accounts—that is, they were changing the shipping address on the bookstore's accounts to their new warehouse.

My friend added that Bulk Orders was also taking the Park Place Bookstore name—since the college would be closing the storefront down.

I didn't know whether to believe this. I checked with Vince Tower, and he confirmed that my best friend's profitable Bulk Orders division would now be calling itself Park Place Bookstore. For the remainder of my storefront's existence I'd have to operate by opening all new vendor accounts using a different name: Park Place Retail. I did not have to redo our awning or website, however.

Park Place Bookstore—a lively branch of Park Place College of Education that for decades had served a hundred-thousand people a year—was preparing to become a buried taproot feeding Linda Lasch's Conquest Academies.

16—A VERY LARGE HOMEWORK ASSIGNMENT: CHAPTER SIX— SEEMINGLY STUPID IMMIGRANTS AND A REVELATION

Jason was waiting in solitude. What else was there to do? His parents were out on a date, and his siblings were nonexistent.

The moon was out, and the stars were shining.

They were so beautiful in the night sky. The sky was so black and they so white. He had never paid attention to them. He had never had time.

Maybe this life he was leading wasn't the right one.

No, it wasn't, that much was clear.

His life had been like a game show. Popularity was all that had mattered. The game show of popularity. Everyone was trying to win, but in the end, you could never really win, because when you apply for a job or a college, nobody cares how much you were liked. So, as in game shows, they give you a boost for a couple of years, but after that, who's the real winner, and the real loser?

"If only I could get out of this situation and start over. Maybe held back a grade wouldn't be so bad after all. But it's too late for that now."

He sighed and shook his head. What was going to happen to him? What was he going to do?

The German immigrants' writing was worse than Alfrate had remembered. For God sakes. Russia will not be a capitalist country in 1918!

Or it's simply not true that when the Indians came to North America on the Mayflower, the Pilgrims gave up their land wholeheartedly.

Or for instance, they couldn't really have thought that they used to bind the feet of plants in China.

Or that Plato was a professional philiopieter.

There were so many of these mistakes it was maddening.

He kept telling these stupid immigrants "to do it right." But that was a capacity which they had not yet gained. So, in a fit of desperate rage, he had said, "Fine, do it yourself. Just, make sure it's right!"

"Fine," was the basic reply. "We'll do it our way." Whatever that meant, Alfrate never found out. He went down to the second floor where his cubicle was, and just hoped the immigrants were doing an OK job.

Jason decided he would try to get his money back. It wouldn't be great if he got held back, but come on, employers don't care about that stuff. And his social life would have to wait.

So, he got up from where he was sitting and trotted over to the computer, turned it on, signed on to America Online, and got into the website www.wedoyourhomeworkforyou.com.

Alfrate was still at his desk doing nothing in particular when he saw Jason. He said, mockingly, "What are you doing here? We'll have your report done on time, OK?"

"About that report. I want it canceled. I want my money back."

Alfrate jerked up his head. "You want this report canceled?" He paused. "I'm sorry, that's impossible right now. It's almost half finished, and at this point, I'm sorry, but we can't call it off."

"Why?" exclaimed Jason.

"I told you, it's half finished. I'm sorry, but that's all there is to it."

"Oh, God," Jason sighed. "All right, I give up. Just have it done on time."

"I'll try," Alfrate said. And they both signed off.

There was nothing for it.

There was nothing Jason could do.

17—OCCUPY PARK PLACE

JANUARY 2014

Last-minute decision: make an appearance at an all-college meet-and-greet with our new president-elect, who'd be taking office July 1st.

I hovered near the coffee machines at the back of the crowded basement cafeteria as Eli Salver spoke to we hundred, milling Park Place staff and faculty.

He dwelt on the recent death of Pete Seeger, the ninety-four-year-old activist folk singer. Salver recalled his mother's love of Seeger's music and politics.

I had a way to connect with him. I waited in line to address Salver directly.

"Thanks for what you said about Pete. My mother played him for me as a kid too. I'm Andy Laties. I run the bookstore. We've been having some real estate problems—"

Salver interrupted, "We're gonna fix that."

This was the last thing I expected.

He was animated. "When I told Carmen I was coming here, she talked my ear off for twenty minutes about the importance of the bookstore. Also, she shops there for her granddaughter."

I understood from reading *The New York Times* that Salver was talking about Carmen Fariña, the incoming New York City Public Schools Chancellor. Carmen Fariña had been appointed by newly elected Mayor Bill de Blasio, the progressive politician who'd been swept into office on the energy of the Occupy Wall Street wave of activism Rebecca and I had participated in two years before.

But I'd read an announcement saying Eli Salver was leaving the number two spot at the public schools; his rise in that bureaucracy had happened under billionaire Mayor Michael Bloomberg, who'd crushed Occupy Wall Street.

So—wouldn't Fariña and Salver be adversaries?

I said the first non-political thing that came to mind: "The bookstore doesn't sell to the New York public schools. We don't have a vendor number with them."

Salver stiffened. "Why not?"

I was referring to information provided me two months prior by my best friend. A teacher had asked at the register if we had a vendor number for accepting public school purchase orders—I'd realized I'd never been trained around this—I'd darted upstairs to ask my friend in Bulk Orders. My friend had said no, Park Place Bookstore didn't have a New York City schools vendor number, and had explained why. Now, I repeated the explanation. "We used to, but they never paid their bills."

Salver seemed annoyed. "We fixed that years ago."

My thirty seconds of face time with my new president were over. He'd offered hope and I'd insulted him.

I retreated to the far coffee machines.

As I glanced again to the front of the cafeteria though, I realized Salver had stepped away from his position greeting the line of staff and faculty. He was now exchanging words with Vince Tower, and with retiring president Wright.

Vince was scanning the cafeteria—and through the crowd his eyes caught mine.

He was looking directly at me with alarm.

*   *   *

I left the cafeteria and climbed the back stairs to the lobby. I threaded the crowd of parents and children reuniting for after-school pickup, past the front desk, through the security gate and sets of doors, turned east, around onto Broadway and into the bookstore.

We were busy with families shopping for birthday presents, required reading, and test prep junk. I wasn't needed at the register, so I headed upstairs.

In the past year-and-a-half I'd bounded up and down these stairs so many times during my hundred-hour weeks that my hip pain drove me to pop Ibuprofen every three hours. My heart-murmur had become a moment-to-moment reality: I halted at the top of the steps to let Old Thump-Bump slow.

I enter the house and notice eight-year-old Sam sitting at the top of the staircase, bent over, holding his head. "Sam? Are you all right?"

"I fell down the steps."

I hurry up to him. There's blood at the center of his forehead.

"What did you bump against?"

Dazed, he can't tell me. It must have been that sharp corner on the pillar at the bottom of the bannister.

"How many steps did you fall?"

He can't tell me.

Chris takes him in for a CAT scan. The test comes back negative: there's no brain injury. Sam will be fine.

"We're gonna fix that."

How had incoming school chancellor Carmen Fariña become so interested in the survival of Park Place Bookstore that she'd promote it for twenty minutes in a meeting with incoming Park Place president Eli Salver?

And why did he plan to grant her wish?

She must have learned of our threatened closure from the burst of media last December. I silently thanked Pamela Paul.

I went to the computer in the bookstore's back office and pulled up the membership database.

Carmen Fariña was an active customer with thousands of dollars in purchases going back before 2000.

I searched the web for combinations of "Carmen Fariña" and "Eli Salver." A *Chalkbeat.org* article appeared. Mayor de Blasio's pledge to bring pre-kindergarten to all children could mean a huge preschool-teacher training contract for Park Place College.

Carmen Fariña was the person who would award this contract.

But there was more: Carmen Fariña had been a professor at Park Place College in the '90s, teaching school leadership.

Eli Salver had been her student.

The Occupy Movement—and Sam's beloved electoral democracy—were saving Park Place Bookstore.

18—A VERY LARGE HOMEWORK ASSIGNMENT: CHAPTER SEVEN—TWO FACE THE MORNING

Alfrate had fallen asleep without noticing it.

"Oh, what time is it?" he said, as he looked at his watch. "Oh, three-fifty, I have to go back to sleep. No that's not three-fifty, that's five-fifty! I have to get up."

So saying, he dragged himself out of his cubicle and over toward the elevator. Maybe he could get an extra twenty minutes of sleep while he was going up to the fourteenth floor in the elevator. But then he thought better of it, and turned toward the stairs, where he dragged himself twelve long stories up to the fourteenth floor.

Those German immigrants better be done, or he'd be in a lot of trouble.

When he got over to Sector H, one of the immigrants stepped out and said, "Here's your stupid paper. We did it our way."

"Whatever," Alfrate said. He looked at the bottom corner of the hundredth page. It said "100" all right. And that's all he looked at.

He rushed down the stairs. By the time he got to the bottom it was six o'clock. He went over to his cubicle and plunked down in front of his computer and waited for Jason to sign on.

Jason's alarm clock went off at six-thirty, and he pressed the snooze button, so he got up at six-forty. But then when he realized what he needed to do, he sprung out of bed and went hurriedly downstairs, and signed on to the Internet site.

Luckily there was no-one else up yet.

"There you are! I thought you'd never come," said Alfrate. "I have your paper."

"How are you going to get it to me?"

"That's easy. We're going to send a messenger to your house."

"Oh?!"

"And we need your address and your name."

"I'm Jason," he said reluctantly, and told him his address. "But are you going to come to my house? Is your office that close?"

"First of all, I'm not going anywhere. A messenger will deliver it. And secondly, yes, our office is close to your house. The report will be there in forty minutes. Bye."

"OK, bye."

"You're up this early, baby?" said his mother. She was walking down the stairs, and yawning. She was wearing a bathrobe.

"Good morning, Mom." For the next twenty minutes or so, Jason and his Mom made "friendly chat." Then he had to start getting ready for school.

When he was finished, and ready to go to school, the paper hadn't come.

Only after he had delayed his leaving the house for ten minutes, with dumb excuses, did the messenger arrive. A big white truck pulled up to the side of the house, and just in time, too.

Jason ran out and got the report. He didn't have time to look at it.

He jumped in his parents' car, and he shut the door.

Many thoughts drifted through his head then.

What was going to happen to him after this?

Would he continue to be the popular kid he had always been?

But most of all, was his teacher going to know that he hadn't written the report, and he had cheated?

Ah, well. There was no time to think about that now.

[CURTAIN]

19—OPEN HEART

SIX MONTHS LATER

Rolling down the surgery ward hallway flat on my back in a hospital gown I reviewed for perhaps the last time in my life what had happened.

Our sweetheart lease for the light-filled corner storefront at 107th and Broadway, in a co-op building filled with families, would be signed in three weeks. Our side had won.

But if I died, I would leave Rebecca in a terrible position both personally and professionally. Also, Sarah at age twenty-five—though launched on a promising career as a film editor—would be traumatized.

Yet—paradoxically, the deepest obligation I'd been fulfilling in trying to save Park Place Bookstore was to Sam. When I'd received that forwarded email from Sarah announcing the opening for store manager, through the unpleasantness of my inherited staff's resentment, always I'd been hearing Sam's voice in my ear. Now, even if I died, Eli Salver would see the store's move through. He had motivations of his own, thank goodness: he'd decided that saving Park Place Bookstore would be his first act as president; this would go along with bookselling outreach to the public schools.

The new Park Place would be Sam's Bookstore.

The hospital gurney reached metal double doors. The orderly who'd been propelling me onward reached ahead and pushed. From my reclined viewpoint, I saw a large room full of machines and—it seemed—crowded with people. Were they all waiting just for me?

A smiling woman in white was approaching, holding a large syringe. She took my arm. I thought, "If Sam can die, I can die." I felt comfort at the realization I would be joining him in death—not leaving him alone anymore, though he had gone first, which had been the wrong order to do this.

From Sarah's room come the voices of fifteen-year-old Sarah and seventeen-year-old Sam. I poke my head in; they're just hanging out.

I ask if, considering the troubles of the world and the travails of life, they're glad they were born.

Startled—in unison—they reply, "Yes!"

Sam would tell me I should live.

20—CELL VS. SOUL: ON UNDERSTANDING PERSUASION

BY SAMUEL LATIES, AGED THIRTEEN

CELL: What would you call living?

SOUL: The inner consciousness of man, which is the soul.

CELL: I must respect your views my friend, but to me it seems that the inner consciousness of man was not given to us by God, but evolved, through trial and error.

SOUL: I am sorry, my friend but I must also respectfully disagree. You see it is, in my view, impossible for this process to have taken place. How could we who have such broad depth of thought, who can contemplate what life is, who can imagine and dream such wondrous things, how can such a being that can perform these actions have come from an ape?

CELL: I can see your line of reasoning, but it is to no avail, for there is no great proof that stands behind your thoughts. All that you say are words of your imagination; evolution is the only possibility that can be shown true. Humans have believed in divine gods and spirits for upwards of ten thousand years. Hundreds of gods have been embraced by tens of millions each. How can your one faith be true when it is only one of hundreds?

SOUL: The soul is a belief of not one faith, but of many, for almost all the people of the world past and present have believed—understood—that body is more than flesh and bone; it is composed of the inner self, which is the soul. How can you presume that billions of people worldwide uniting in one common view can be wrong? They have had this view for as long as human beings have existed; it is inside them, it is them, it has been enrooted deep in their bones, they are born with this inner understanding.

CELL: But I reiterate that you have not a shred of proof to back up your case. You talk of inner feeling. Inner feeling, yes it is important in life, but it is no proof. Waking up one day and saying "I know something new" without being taught is utterly ridiculous.

SOUL: You have defied understanding. Are you to tell me that the human being is made of meat, that our consciousness is just a by-product of genetic mutation, that we are nothing but mimes?

CELL: And are you to tell me that the human was placed on Earth by an immortal flying thing that claims to be superior to all others by divine right? This 'divine' creature must have had a foul fondness for cockroaches, a fondness that exceeds all limits of imagination.

SOUL: Your insolence has no bounds. You say that the human being is just an instruction manual and operating system of meat, just a meaningless bunch of meat. How can you think this?

CELL: Your stupidity is unmatched in the entire cosmos. You idiotic pig.

SOUL: I am not the idiotic pig; you are the idiotic pig. No you are worse than an idiotic pig; you are idiotic fly excrement.

CELL: How dare you, you piece of....

Our humanity gives us the gift of option. To respect your neighbors' opinions as if they were your own shows not only respect, but increases the chances of your opinions being accepted, for a person with a higher level of maturity is more likely to be correct. But to force your views on another is to show no respect, and thus your own views must be questioned, for they come from someone of less maturity.

21—SAM'S COSMIC RIDDLE

MIDDAY, AUGUST 17, 2010
ASKED AT RIVER VALLEY COUNSELING CENTER

What did the ostrich say when the frog asked him why he crossed the road?

OSTRICH: *What road?*

ACKNOWLEDGMENTS

Heartfelt thanks to teachers and counselors who appreciated Sam and encouraged his writing, especially Ken Danford of North Star, Dr. Meredith Gould, Larry Levitt of River Valley Counseling Center, Jeff Peters and Kathy Siavelis of Near North Montessori, Jennifer Ralph of Amherst Regional High School, BJ Richards of BJ's Kids, Dr. Shoshana Sokoloff, and Frances Vig of Chicago Waldorf School.

Thanks to the Park Placers who appear in this book, most of them pseudonymously. It can't be easy to work with an author who periodically mentions that he's writing a book about what's happening right now. I'm sorry if I hurt any feelings. We were all under pressure and doing our best.

Thanks to the thousands of devoted Park Place Bookstore supporters, many of whom became personal friends.

Thanks to my colleagues at Eric Carle Museum of Picture Book Art, especially Eliza Brown, and Barbara Carle.

Thanks to friends from whom I received valuable advice about this hybrid manuscript: John Ayers, Mira Bartok, Laura Kelsey, Veronica Liu, Katherine Seger, and Dan Simon.

Thanks to the family members and friends who played a supporting role in this book's events and creation, in particular, Isaac Bloom, Christine Bluhm, Margaret Bluhm, Charles Catania, Claire Laties Davis, Susan Davis, Nancy Laties Feresten, Nere Kapiteni, David Laties, Martha Laties, Sarah Laties, Sylvan Migdal, Jessica Spears, and my dad, Victor Laties, who kept urging, "Write another book!"

Thanks especially to my son and co-author Samuel Laties, for his love of the world, his acute sense of humor, and his inspiring vision for a humane future. Sam discarded many of his writings but luckily, he spared some of the best.

Finally, endless gratitude to my soulmate, Rebecca Migdal. As George Lakoff suggests—and as we affirmed in our wedding vows—"Love is a collaborative work of art."

NOTES

Epigraph. Anne Sexton, "To a Friend Whose Work Has Come to Triumph," *The Complete Poems* ([1960] Boston: Houghton Mifflin Company, 1981).

1—BIRTH

Page 1. Samuel Laties, "Birth" (Chicago: Near North Montessori Grade 6, 2001).

2—SING, GODDESS

Page 4. Sylvan Migdal, *Curvy* (Chicago, IL: Iron Circus, 2019).

Page 5. "the only words he'd spoken"
Books Sam read aloud August 2009 to August 2010:
David Copperfield, Charles Dickens; *Candide,* Voltaire; *Walden,* Henry David Thoreau; *Oliver Twist,* Charles Dickens; *War and Peace,* Leo Tolstoy; *Les Miserables,* Victor Hugo; *The Wolves of Willoughby Chase,* Joan Aiken; *One Hundred Years of Solitude,* Gabriel Garcia Marquez; *The Count of Monte Cristo,* Alexandre Dumas; *A People's History of the United States,* Howard Zinn; *The Adventures of Huckleberry Finn,* Mark Twain; *Palace Walk,* Naguib Mahfouz

Page 6. Charles Dickens, *David Copperfield* ([1850] New York: Penguin, 2004).

Page 7. Homer, *The Iliad and the Odyssey,* Translated by Robert Fagles ([800 BCE] New York: Penguin, 1999).

3—MEMOIR OF A NIGHTTIME FANTASY

Page 9. Samuel Laties, "Memoir of a Nighttime Fantasy" (Amherst, MA: Amherst High School Grade 10, 2004).

5—A VERY LARGE HOMEWORK ASSIGNMENT

Page 19. Samuel Laties, "A Boy, A Web Site Company, and a Very Large Homework Assignment" (Chicago: Near North Montessori Grade 5, 1999).

6—INTO A MAELSTROM

Page 23. Andrew Laties, *Rebel Bookseller: Why Indie Businesses Represent Everything You Want to Fight For—From Free Speech to Buying Local to Building Communities* ([2005] New York: Seven Stories Press, 2011).

Page 26. Robert Kraus, *Leo the Late Bloomer*, Illustrated by Jose Aruego (New York: Harper and Row, 1971).

Page 27. William Ayers, *To Teach: The Journey of a Teacher* (New York: Teachers College Press, 1993).

8—PENT-UP FORCES

Page 36. Barry Moser, *The Holy Bible: King James Edition / The Pennyroyal Caxton Bible* (New York: Viking Studio, 1999).

Page 38. Samuel Laties, "My Schooling" (Chicago: Clonlara School application, 2001).

Page 43. "books on my shelves"
James Thurber and E.B. White, *Is Sex Necessary? Or, Why You Feel the Way You Do* ([1929] New York: HarperCollins, 2004); Alison Bechdel, *Fun Home* (New York: Houghton Mifflin Harcourt, 2007) 214; Ganzeer, "Back Cover," *World War 3 Illustrated #43: Expression! Repression! Revolution!* (New York: World War 3 Illustrated, 2012); Rebecca Migdal, *Cock Robin's Wedding* ([2009] New York: Mythoprint, 2018).

Page 44. Rebecca Migdal, "In Praise of Whistleblowers," *World War 3 Illustrated #43: Expression! Repression! Revolution!* (New York: World War 3 Illustrated, 2012) 60-65.

Page 44. Rebecca Migdal, "Village Days," *Bohemians*, ed. Paul Buhle (New York: Verso, 2014) 69-92.

Page 48. Leo Tolstoy, *War and Peace,* Translated by Richard Pevear and Larissa Volokhonsky ([1865] New York: Knopf Doubleday, 2011).

10—DOUBLE CONSCIOUSNESS

Page 57. Gabriel Garcia Marquez, *One Hundred Years of Solitude,* Trans. Gregory Rabassa ([1967] New York: Harper Perennial, 2006), Alexandre Dumas, *The Count of Monte Cristo,* Translated by Robin Buss ([1844] New York: Penguin Classics, 2003).

Page 58. *Julie Andrews' Treasury for all Seasons,* Edited by Julie Andrews and Emma Walton Hamilton (New York: Little, Brown Books, 2012).

Page 60. Samuel Laties, "Baby F. Huey and the World" (Chicago, 2000).

Page 64. Samuel Laties, "Rescue," *Connected—Poems by the Poetry Workshop for Kids,* Edited by Ellen Palmer (Chicago: The Poetry Workshop for Kids, 1998).

13—I WON'T BET MY SOUL TO THE DEVIL

Page 75. Julie Andrews and Emma Walton Hamilton, *The Very Fairy Princess Follows Her Heart* (New York: Little Brown Books for Young Readers, 2013).

Page 81. Hillary Clinton, *It Takes a Village and Other Lessons Children Teach Us* (New York: Simon & Schuster, 1996).

Page 82. "We started with"
Raffi, *Spider on the Floor,* Illustrated by Bill Russell (New York: Knopf, 2002); Byron Barton, *Dinosaurs, Dinosaurs* (New York: HarperCollins, 1993); Robert Louis Stevenson, *A Child's Garden of Verses,* Illustrated by Tasha Tudor ([1885] New York: Simon & Schuster, 1999); Adam Rubin, *Dragons Love Tacos* (New York: Dial Books for Young Readers, 2012); Alice Schertle, *Little Blue Truck Leads the Way,* Illustrated by Jill McElmurry (New York: Houghton Mifflin Harcourt, 2009).

Page 93. "article for the North Star newsletter"
Samuel Laties, "Sam Laties," *Liberated Learners,* Volume IV, Issue 7 (Amherst, MA: Northstar—Self-Directed Learning for Teens, 2003) 2-3. www.northstarteens.org. (Text slightly condensed.)

See also: Kenneth Danford, *Learning is Natural, School is Optional: The North Star approach to offering teens a head-start on life* (Sunderland, MA: Golden Door Press, 2019).

Page 94. Ken Kesey, *Once Flew Over the Cuckoo's Nest* (New York: Viking, 1962).

Page 100. Samuel Laties, "What People Like About the Class and What They Would Like Changed," The Jeff's Class Tribune, Volume 1, Issue 3 (Chicago: *The Jeff's Class Tribune,* 1999).

Page 102. Arnold Lobel, *Grasshopper on the Road* (New York: Harper and Row, 1978).

Page 102. Samuel Laties, "My Schooling" (Chicago: Clonlara School application, 2001).

Page 104. "Reading and Writing Institutes" https://readingandwritingproject.org/services/institutes

Page 108. Samuel Laties, "Day in Review" (Amherst, MA: private journal, 2006).

Page 109. Robert Graves, *I, Claudius* ([1934] New York: Vintage, 1989).

Page 109. Neil Gaiman, Jon Klassen, Lemony Snicket, *The Dark* (New York: HarperCollins, 2013).

Page 110. "Park Place-inspired books"
Ruth Krauss, *The Carrot Seed*, Illustrated by Crockett Johnson (New York: Harper and Row, 1945), Crockett Johnson, *Harold and the Purple Crayon* (New York: Harper and Row, 1955), Margaret Wise Brown, *Goodnight Moon*, Illustrated by Clement Hurd (New York: Harper and Row, 1947). Maurice Sendak, *Where the Wild Things Are* (New York: Harper and Row, 1963). Leonard Marcus, *Golden Legacy: The Story of Golden Books* (New York: Golden Books, 2017).

15—MALPRACTICE

Page 117. Diane Ravitch, *The Death and Life of the Great American School System* (New York: Basic Books, 2010).

20—CELL VS. SOUL

Page 137. Samuel Laties, "Cell Vs. Soul: On Understanding Persuasion" (Chicago: Near North Montessori, Grade 6, 2001).

ACKNOWLEDGMENTS

Page 144. "Love is a collaborative work of art"
George Lakoff and Mark Johnson, *Metaphors We Live By* (Chicago, IL: University of Chicago Press) 139.

SAMUEL LATIES attended BJ's Kids, Chicago Waldorf School, Near North Montessori, North Star, Amherst Regional High School, Holyoke Community College and Greenfield Community College. For two years, he published The Jeff's Class Tribune, *documenting class events and featuring his original fiction.* He loved taking long walks and climbing to high places.

ANDREW LATIES managed Park Place Bookstore from 2012 to 2017. He co-founded Easton Book Festival, Book & Puppet Company, Vox Pop, The Children's Bookstore, Chicago Children's Museum Store, and Eric Carle Museum Bookstore. He shared the 1987 Women's National Book Association Pannell Award for bringing children and books together. His *Rebel Bookseller: Why Indie Businesses Represent Everything You Want to Fight For—From Free Speech to Buying Local to Building Communities* won the 2006 Independent Publisher Award and is available in a 2nd edition from Seven Stories Press.

www.ingramcontent.com/pod-product-compliance
Lightning Source LLC
Chambersburg PA
CBHW070606010526
44118CB00012B/1456